How to Stop Wars and Save the World

Lessons in Negotiation, Settlement and Leadership

Bob Worden, Esq.

ACKNOWLEDGMENTS

This book is the culmination of the generosity of many people, too numerous to mention, whose kindness and guidance enabled me to move forward with work which was rewarding and enjoyable. I want to specifically thank everyone in the Worden family who contributed, especially Molly Worden, editing the very first draft and encouraging me to move forward. I also want to thank Jack Hipp for his insights and the many conversations we shared about history.

TABLE OF CONTENTS

LESSONS

> *"Every man seeks peace by waging war, but no man wages war by seeking peace…In interrupting the peace, men only seek a different peace that suits them better."*

> – St. Augustine

FOREWORD: Russia and Ukraine

> *Here we go again…*
> *When's it gonna end?*
> *How many stones do we have to line up*
> *Before we understand?*
> *Caught up, drawing lines on a paper*
> *At the price of the blood in the sand…*
>
> *Right back where we've always been*
> *These excuses are wearing thin…*
>
> *Can't decide, but you've got to win*
> *We're all the same, but you're not my friend*
> *So, what's the reason for this again?"*

> –from "Wargasm,"
> A Song by Billy Strings

How many of us want to learn about what happened in wars? We hear snippets about wars here and there, but our sources of information are either too simple or too complex, so we say, "Oh well," and accept that this is just one more subject that we will never understand. At the same time, the current state of the world creates anxiety, and we have the feeling of wanting to do something to help our world become less scary, to obtain more stability and security. The main purpose of this book is to help you learn the stories of three American wars as painlessly as possible. By reading about these wars, you can learn three things at once: 1) the mistakes leaders made which led to wars; 2) the actions our leaders should take going forward, to avoid war, where it is possible to do so; 3) negotiation fundamentals and settlement techniques to assist in resolving any conflict or dispute.

Although I am no military or political expert, my work as a mediator and lawyer over many years trained me to analyze and simplify conflicts and then explain them in writing to ordinary people. The genesis of this book was sparked from reading a number of histories of American wars and recognizing how little about the situations behind these wars is taught in American schools. Mistakes in negotiation and the failure of leadership are common factors which led to the fighting, much of which was counterproductive.

The conflicts which led to three American wars reveal how effective negotiations could have helped leaders of nations avoid fighting these wars, or at least, show how these leaders could have ended these wars earlier. This book will help you to learn the stories of what caused the Revolutionary, Civil and Vietnam wars, without having to read the historical details most people do not need nor care to know.

The true stories of these American wars are much more interesting than the filtered information taught in high school history courses. You will see similarities in the situations of these wars to today's political conflicts. At the same time, you will develop an understanding of negotiation and settlement principles. These skills should help you improve your own outcomes in resolving conflicts. You will also learn the basics of negotiation and settlement, and how effective leaders can make the correct decisions to help their people end their conflicts, or at least reduce their conflicts and move forward.

By understanding the situations which resulted in fighting wars, you can learn how to help prevent unnecessary wars, and help end current wars. Our political leaders need encouragement to reach negotiated solutions, rather than fight. Knowledge and understanding of past mistakes will guide you to choose leaders to make the best decisions, preventing unnecessary death and destruction to soldiers and civilians, and helping everyone to move forward to a brighter future.

Wrong thinking led to fighting these American wars, and wrong thinking stood in the way of settling them. We need to choose leaders who are open-minded and are willing to listen to the lessons of the past, leaders who understand the means and techniques to achieve settlement. Selecting the best political leaders is essential to maintaining peace and resolving conflicts between nations. Together, we can stop the fighting and save the world.

Schools often teach history in a way that implies that wars have always ended the way they were supposed to end, as though Fate had already determined the outcome of a war. Nothing could be farther from the truth. After you appreciate the facts behind the fighting, you may agree that these three American wars took place because of bad decision-making and bad luck.

If sensible leaders negotiate whenever possible, they can avoid fighting wars. When negotiation fails, leaders must do everything possible to win wars quickly, when the circumstances require fighting.

It is hard to understand the mistakes which led to past wars without being familiar with their stories. It is difficult to know what to do when a war is imminent, and the combatants are hiding information from each other. Understanding the past is the best way to find out what we need to know to avoid the world blowing up. What actions lead to peace and prosperity? How can we determine if our political leaders are being truthful? Which political candidates will make the right decisions for a better future? We must look to past mistakes to avoid making similar mistakes ourselves.

It is important to understand that most wars are settled to end the fighting. How do you motivate your leaders to negotiate early? Once the fighting has begun, how can we reach an agreement to resolve the fighting quickly, saving the lives of soldiers and civilians?

Outcomes of war often depend on the influence of specific individuals. The efforts of just one person may determine who will win and who will lose. One person, at the right place at the right time, can change an outcome for an entire nation, for better or worse.

At the present time, Russia's war with Ukraine rages with death and destruction. This war has the potential to continue to expand and drag more countries into fighting, escalating into world-wide conflict. If the leaders from all sides make the right choices soon, there is a better chance to achieve a lasting settlement between Ukraine and Russia.

Russia's leaders initiated the fighting, their goal to benefit Russia in the long term. As this conflict continues, Russia's leaders may be amenable to accepting a different peace than a peace they would have accepted at the beginning of the fighting. Ukrainian leaders, having had early success in defending their nation, are less likely to agree to as generous a settlement with Russia as might have been accomplished to avoid the war before the war started.

Each side must give something to make a deal to settle this conflict. Both sides must perceive the settlement as fair, or the settlement will not last. As historian Steven Kotkin has said, it is not enough to win a war if victory merely sets the stage for a future conflict. It is more important to win lasting peace.

If there is no settlement between Russia and Ukraine, there will be unbounded destruction of property and loss of life on both sides.

Regardless of which side claims victory, both Ukraine and Russia will end up worse off if fighting continues. When leaders agree to negotiate, with no pre-conditions, assisted by neutral mediators, they are more likely to attain a stable settlement.

An important concept to motivate both Russian leaders and Ukrainian leaders to settle is understanding that luck will play a role which no one can predict. Either side may have good luck or bad luck going forward, potentially changing the conflict, or bringing unforeseen danger, with major consequences.

Both sides must keep open minds about practical solutions which might work. If both sides are serious about avoiding fighting and are willing to make good-faith efforts to fully understand the needs of the other side, this conflict could end sooner than anyone thinks is possible.

One Caveat: To reach a settlement of any dispute, it is important that leaders consider the perspective of their opposition. When both sides accept that settlement usually leads to a better future than what will be obtained by continuing to fight, they are more likely to focus on negotiating to reach common ground.

Russia began its aggression, calculating that it had overwhelming power to win. Overwhelming power does not rely on reason, ethics, or morality. A nation with overwhelming power does not need to convince, apologize, or argue. Using overwhelming power can achieve victory, although often, the victors find that winning is easier than retaining the gains won after the fighting is over.

The voters in a nation like America, having so many kind, humane and caring people, need to understand how important it is for the American military to possess the best weapons to defend the American way of life, to minimize the risk of conquest by a brutal nation wielding superior weapons. A new brutal regime will quickly destroy the kind, humane and caring people, along with their government. In order to successfully negotiate for its best solutions, America must retain its power to dominate when waging war, and at the same time, apply American military power as a last alternative, only when necessary.

PART 1: Negotiation and Settlement Fundamentals

"What is war? I believe that half the people that talk about war have not the slightest idea of what it is. In a short sentence it may be summed up to be the combination and concentration of all the horrors, atrocities, crimes, and sufferings of which human nature on this globe is capable....I confess when I think of the tremendous perils into which unthinking men—men who do not intend to fight themselves—are willing to drag or to hurry this country, I am amazed how they can trifle with interests so vast, and consequences so much beyond their calculation.

– John Bright, British Statesman, 1853

American voters typically rely upon the news media to form their opinions. News stories and editorials dispense information highlighting conflicts, exaggerating the importance of everyday's events, which is their way of generating advertising revenues. Most reporters are not looking to achieve consensus and solve problems. Stories may contain inciting misinformation geared to point people in one direction or the other. It is ironic that even though the Internet provides tremendous access to better information, there is a surplus of unreliable information repeated *ad nauseam,* much of which is not useful.

It would be helpful if reporters made fewer attacks and focused their questions on clarifying situations. But more often than not, news reporters support a politician by asking "softball" questions to trigger answers crafted in advance to garner political support. Other reporters seek to harm the reputations of public figures by flinging loaded questions, seeking to embarrass or confuse. Even when they seek information, often news reporters are unfamiliar with the lessons of history and lack the skill to pin down slick politicians who duck questions and refuse to address real concerns.

Better than relying on news reporters, voters can learn the lessons of the past themselves. Readers can discover gems of wisdom mined from reliable sources by talented historians. The curious can easily find excellent lectures for free online by writers such as those noted in the Resources section of this book. Paying attention to better sources of information will help voters develop a deeper understanding of key issues. Knowledgeable voters are more likely to choose elected officials who will make good decisions, or failing that, these voters will choose better leaders the next time.

The stories in this book are based upon the writings of top historians who have spent their lives studying past conflicts. Although they have done challenging work to explain the causes of these wars, and identify the bad actors who made things worse, readers must spend a great deal of time and thought to dig through these important sources of information. The historians' perspective allows them to write about what happened in greater detail, usually with the goal of providing comprehensive information about wars for all sorts of purposes.

In contrast, this book provides the key stories of these three American wars in easily understood language, its sole focus to show how leaders might have avoided wars and ended wars earlier. In all of these wars, leaders from both sides missed opportunities for pre-war settlement or earlier settlement once the wars were raging. Leaders failed to begin serious negotiations before the wars started or failed to grasp settlement opportunities presented during the fighting.

Although the design of this book is to provide only those facts needed to understand these wars, detailed histories of these three American wars related in other books contain stories about particular battles. Severe weather, misunderstanding, misinformation, and unfounded assumptions often affected the outcome of these battles. There was no way for either side to know what was going to happen before the fighting started. Battles became turning points and changed the outcomes of the conflicts. Those detailed histories found in other books demonstrate that fighting is unpredictable and that no leader should assume easy victory in any conflict.

Along with readable stories about these wars, this book also contains vignettes describing the personalities and abilities of key people who made big differences in the outcomes of the wars. The importance of these individuals could not be known in advance. Yet, their contributions had massive effects. Individual action is unpredictable, part of the "luck" which should motivate all sides to negotiate, if possible. The inescapable uncertainty of the future requires all sides to embrace negotiated outcomes, rather than proceed with risky gambles.

Mediators assist in settlement negotiations to resolve conflicts. Using these settlement experts ensures that the leaders for each side will understand their potential negative outcomes and appreciate the extent of uncertainty inherent in fighting. Even when provided with the best advice, leaders often reject negotiation, later learning the hard way that their expectations of success were too optimistic.

It is important to know how human psychology comes into play. Like the rest of us, the leaders in the world started out as babies. If they were lucky enough to develop in a stable, supportive environment, they matured and learned to make rational choices. When leaders come from unstable backgrounds, they may react to conflict less rationally and more emotionally, therefore, likely to make uninformed choices.

Complicating matters is the great variation in behaviors, motives, and personalities of people, due to a combination of genetics and experiences. Uncertainty abounds in attempting to predict the motives, methods, and choices of any individual.

As we mature, most of us learn not to incite unnecessary fights to obtain what we want. How others think, talk, and behave are key factors to consider, in assessing our best course to negotiate with them. Experience has taught us that we might be injured in any fight. We learned to bargain back and forth with others, to solve our problems with a minimum of damage to ourselves, neither wanting nor needing to interfere with the goals of others any more than necessary.

When there is conflict in a family, it may be helpful to have a neutral relative, friend, or therapist present when people are upset, to help keep everyone centered, to focus on solutions to the conflict. People caught up in emotion need someone to remind them of the costs and the downsides of continuing quarrels. They need someone to remind them of the benefits of reaching an agreement.

All people need resources. Who does not want good food, a nice place to live, and security? Yet, there is competition for these resources. To survive, some people become driven to succeed, some enjoy stealing, and some devote themselves to a religion. Life does not limit how any particular person will act, although all people receive rewards and disappointments, much depending on luck, as well as their genetics, their environment, and the choices they make.

Some leaders are bullies, applying force to get what they want from others. Bullies learned to fight, or at least to threaten, looking for results they find gratifying. Other people avoid conflict and freely give to accommodate others. If conflict-avoidant people become leaders, they do not stay leaders for long, as they eventually relinquish control to others who will not shy away from conflict. Placing a high value on keeping the peace, conflict-avoidant people accept losing power and resources, even when it is not in their best interest to give in.

Bullying leaders compete to obtain resources for themselves and their people, aggressively seeking domination and control, not caring if they destroy others' ability to pursue their own paths toward happiness. These aggressive leaders see the world as a "zero-sum" game, a world in which someone else must be the one to lose if the aggressive leader is going to win. Aggressors tend to push hard, and more often than not, the recipient of the aggression gives in. But sometimes, aggressors push too hard and suffer major losses. They may produce their own destruction, not recognizing that others will fight back hard when negotiation proves fruitless.

Convincing leaders to change their thinking requires choosing the right arguments or producing the right evidence to convince them to find a better solution through settlement. Mediators are experts in helping opposing sides reach an agreement. Even when leaders are certain about their best outcome, they can be uncertain about choosing a path to obtain that outcome. It is naïve to think that leaders, given a chance, will agree on everything and get along. It is not the way the world works. It is attractive to wish for such a world to exist, as hoping for no conflict can alleviate anxiety. The reality of the human experience is that conflicts always arise and can be difficult to resolve. The best way to alleviate anxiety is to face conflict and directly address the problems.

Leaders can have unpleasant personalities and engage in counter-productive tactics, causing negotiations to break down. Mediators usually guide leaders to remain patient and to keep their focus on problem-solving. Difficult personalities and questionable tactics of the opposition are mere distractions. It is important for leaders to remain calm, and to be clear about their sides' needs and goals when faced with unpleasant behavior by the opposition. Settlement is more difficult to achieve when large numbers of people and groups are in conflict.

Under the American republican form of democracy, voters cannot directly control their state and federal governments. By voting for their political candidates, Americans have the opportunity to control which representatives will lead their governments. American voters need to know what their leaders are doing to protect the people's lives, liberties, and abilities to pursue happiness. Possessing sufficient knowledge of past mistakes of the leaders who came before, voters may better judge when their current leaders are acting foolishly. Voters may make their opinions known, either by sending requests to their elected representatives, or failing that, to vote for better leaders who demonstrate superior abilities to choose a good path, enhancing the quality of voters' lives going forward.

Thomas Jefferson said that Americans do not need "Kings, Priests and Nobles" to guide them. Americans need only to look at their own capacity to reason and use common sense to make the right choices. Jefferson would probably agree that it is important for Americans to understand what has happened in the past to be better able to judge and make decisions. If Americans have little knowledge regarding the mistakes of the past, how will they recognize when the poor choices by their leaders are taking them down the risky roads of conflict?

Wars should be ended at the earliest possible opportunity with solutions that provide long-term stability. Knowledgeable, rational debate will help the American people reach a consensus about what needs to happen going forward. Where war is inevitable, or where war has already started, the voters possess the power to pressure American leaders to settle wars as early as possible, preserving the best chances for all sides to benefit going forward.

While negotiating, there is no benefit gained from losing patience or complaining about someone's behavior, unless that person's behavior is so grossly offensive that settlement discussions will end if the offending behavior continues. Politely pointing out the offending behavior and calmly requesting that it stop is the best tactic to prevent recurrences.

Good negotiation avoids triggering negative emotions of the opposition unnecessarily. Settlement is easier to achieve when the participants do not project animosity towards people on the opposite side of the table who may have a different take on what should happen to end the dispute. It is important to avoid raising voices and showing angry faces. Personal conflict takes the focus away from solving the problems at hand. "Lose-Lose" frequently happens when animosity gets in the way of rational discussion.

A mediator looks for settlements which provide each party with an opportunity to obtain value for their side. The mediator has to stand in the shoes of each side to try to help them reach an agreement. Mediators do not have the right to decide the best outcome. Each side has the final say in their own choices. Therefore, when analyzing the benefits negotiation could have produced to resolve past wars, we must judge how close each side came to obtaining what they had wanted to obtain before the fighting started. If that side failed to obtain what they were looking for, we look to determine whether mistakes made by one side led to their poor outcome, or whether unforeseen events and bad luck provided the poor result.

Once a mediator fully understands the negotiating position of each side, the mediator has private discussions with each side. The mediator discloses only the information that each side has approved to be disclosed to their opposition. With a neutral go-between, communication problems are less likely. Without a neutral go-between, due to fear of demonstrating weakness or fear of disclosing secrets, opposing sides may fail to accurately communicate their own concerns. They may not listen to, or attempt to understand the opposition's concerns, impeding any chances for an agreed settlement.

Having no stake in the outcome, a mediator usually sees paths to settlement more clearly than the opposing sides. When the mediator meets with each side privately, the mediator can persuasively voice the ways that the current landscape of the conflict could change, if not resolved. Even when a possible bad outcome is remote, mediators need to discuss an unlikely bad outcome, should there be a failure to reach a settlement. Just because a bad outcome is unlikely does not mean that it will not happen.

Parts of a dispute can often be resolved quickly. A mediator focuses on identifying items upon which both sides might agree. Often, the basis of a conflict comes down to reaching a compromise on a few key items. With give and take, a comprehensive settlement agreement can accommodate the needs of all.

Cool, rational explanation is the best method for relaying the important points of one side to the other side, while at the same time, a mediator must be careful to avoid stirring up bad feelings, to gently help leaders understand the benefits of reaching an agreement in a particular situation. Reliable information, presented in a palatable way to leaders who keep open minds, usually results in those leaders making the right choices for their side.

Leaders who ignore the weaknesses of their own position compound the risks for their side going forward. Resistance to change is often costly. Listening to information with an open mind includes the willingness to recognize the best course going forward, which may require accepting that one's former beliefs may no longer be supportable. Unavoidable truths reveal themselves eventually, so it is better to accept them, rather than pretend they do not exist.

Leaders may resist changing their prior stance with regard to a conflict, to avoid the psychological pain of accepting that their past actions have proven to be mistakes. Continuing the fight with a losing strategy is likely to make matters even worse.

Overconfidence often leads people to underestimate the risk of a bad outcome. Psychological testing has shown, for example, that most people think they are smarter than average, and most people think that they are better looking than average. Simple mathematics tells us that everybody cannot be better than average. By definition, a sizable number of people must be wrong about themselves. They may also be overconfident about their chances for success fighting wars or winning battles. Overconfidence was widespread in these American Wars. Deflating overconfidence is often the key to reaching a settlement.

Leaders can be deaf to negatives. Often, they do not want to project weakness by deviating from their prior positions. Unrealistic expectations of one or both sides can prevent settlement. When both sides entrench around a conflict, it may be impossible to achieve a settlement. This is particularly true when leaders claim that a deity is on their side. These types of claims move the dispute away from rational appraisal, allowing strong emotion to prevent reaching an agreement.

Worst of all is when one side commits treachery or inhumane acts against the other. Outrage from the recipients prevents settlement, due to loss of trust and extreme emotion. Achieving a settlement depends on each side trusting each other to live up to any agreement that may be reached.

PART 2: The American Revolution

"There was never a good war, or a bad peace."

— Benjamin Franklin, 1783

Whether it was possible to avoid the war of the American Revolution is an attractive question. What did the British assume would happen, which did not happen? What did Americans assume would happen, which did not happen? What happened that nobody expected?

From the beginning, the British government sowed the seeds for its difficulties in its American colonies by requiring these colonies to fund and administer their own local colonial governments. Rather than Britain expending its own funds and personnel to create a strong, British-run government in these colonies, Britain instead gave exclusive charters to private British trading companies to profit from investing in establishing these colonies. British trading companies financed the transportation and funding for British subjects to settle in North America. This was the most economical way for the British government to obtain the benefits of American trade. As is true in most people's experience, doing something the most economical way often creates problems later. The British placed the private chartering companies and the settlers in these colonies in a situation where they had to "sink or swim" if they wanted to survive.

Their successful self-reliance created expectations for colonial leaders going forward. Control over their own local governments fostered expectations of continuing independence as the colonies grew and prospered. Expectations are often hard to change. Colonial leaders became accustomed to wielding the power to make choices and decisions for themselves and their people.

After fitful starts in the beginning, the number of British citizens inhabiting the colonies increased, mostly from trading for furs with Native Americans. When the early settlers found that they could grow tobacco in Virginia, colonial trade quickly increased. The American colonies were soon competing with each other for profits. Britain was happy to see friction appear between the different American colonies, which gave Britain opportunities to better exploit each colony. The American colonies had developed differently, and each colony operated differently than the others.

The Dutch had founded their colony of New Netherlands, occupying from the east coast of North America from Cape May, New Jersey to Rhode Island, emigrating to preserve their religious freedom. They were mostly Protestant and had come under attack by Spanish Catholics in the Netherlands. The capital of the Dutch colony was called New Amsterdam, later to become New York, after the British successfully usurped this Dutch colony, thereby creating a continuity of British colonies extending along the east coast from New England through Virginia.

The Dutch in America prized religious freedom and were tolerant of other immigrants seeking the freedom to practice different religions in their colony. Already a major trade center, New Amsterdam became a melting pot, where eight different languages were spoken by the time the British took control of the colony and changed its name to New York. Business continued to thrive as there was little government restriction or limitation upon trade by either the Dutch or the British. Each inhabitant possessed the freedom to work and profit as they saw fit, regardless of their color or ethnicity.

When Britain took possession of the New Netherlands, British leaders understood that allowing the Dutch settlers and other inhabitants to remain would help to increase trade. The British provided Dutch merchants and their ships continued access to New York Harbor, growing the financial strength of this new British colony. The local people continued to enjoy freedom of religion and a pro-trade government. One hundred years later, being long accustomed to unrestricted trade, the leaders of New York would resist British attempts to obtain a greater share of colonial profits.

Britain's leaders intended that no single American colony had sufficient power to threaten British control. The British believed that the conflicts between the colonies would prevent the colonies from unifying and challenging Britain.

Under any circumstances, given the separate powers of each colony, political leaders of each American colony would have to give up a degree of their power to be able to unite with other American colonies. None of the colonial leaders wanted to give up any of their power as each colony prospered. Over the century before the War of the Revolution, it would take a great deal of British mismanagement and pig-headedness to motivate colonial leaders to band together to fight against Britain.

The American Revolution which resulted was unusual as a political revolution because the aim of the colonials was to *preserve* their existing way of life. Most rebellions within nations before that time arose when economic conditions deteriorated, causing the common people to overthrow their government, making a choice that it was better to fight against their own government than to starve, to suffer abuse and neglect. When people are starving and oppressed, risking their lives seems to be the only choice. But in America, the Colonials had little to complain about their British connections until Britain attempted to squeeze additional profits from the colonies. The desire to maintain economic control fueled the Revolution, as British leaders asserted the right to rule their colonies in the manner which they believed was best. The repeated application of the heavy hand of Britain eventually drove the Colonials to revolution.

The political situation in America had not gone unnoticed by the rest of the world. Once colonial leaders declared independence from Britain, monarchs from around the globe watched closely to see how the American gambit for freedom would play out. European monarchs doubted that the common American people, working together, had the ability to govern themselves. They felt that the Americans lacked adequate education, intellectual ability, and self-control to effectively govern their own nation. How could common people negotiate with foreign leaders? How could common people wield the power to create and maintain the armies and navies required to provide security from foreign influence and invasion? How could people of humble origins, without formal education, manage the reins of power?

Worse, if a new government by common people could be successful in America, would common people of other nations overthrow their monarchs as a consequence? The British aristocracy predicted that democratic government by common people would quickly end in mob rule, chaos, and anarchy, leading to the destruction of the new American government. When the war of the American Revolution started, the leaders of the nations of the world waited and watched for what most believed would be the downfall of the United States. (Today, it still gives one pause to think that leaders of several nations continue to wait and hope for the demise and destruction of the American government.)

During our school days growing up in America, we learned a simple maxim that America became independent of Britain after the American Revolution, due to Britain taxing Americans without having provided political representation for the interests of the American colonials. As is detailed below, misinformation received and blindly accepted by the British leaders in power was the primary cause of the war of the American Revolution. Reliance on unreliable information by closed-minded British leaders created overconfidence, which was the key cause of Britain's losses in America.

The British government did not want to impose taxes on British subjects within Britain to fund the start-up of colonies in America. Britain was already spending too much money fighting wars in Europe. It was politically and practically expedient to allow private British business interests to take on the risk of financing colonization, in return for the opportunity for the private corporations to make huge profits by exploiting the natural resources of North America.

Britain had been slower than other European nations to seek wealth by forming colonies in the Americas. Portugal and Spain had taken the lead in colonization and had become fabulously wealthy by dispossessing their colonies of gold, silver, and jewels, as well as establishing trade. Over time, Portugal became less powerful as Spain became stronger. Other European countries were fearful of Spain's power and were careful to colonize in places where Spain had no interest. For this reason, France decided to colonize Canada, to obtain wealth from trading with the Native Americans for furs. Britain chose to colonize the east coast of North America, between the Spanish colony in Florida and France's Canadian colonization.

The Spanish and French ran their colonies using top-down authority and decision-making from their monarchs and ministers. Both nations had large bureaucracies, which were inefficient. The Spanish and French leaders dominated their colonies with fear, making decisions for their Colonials, with little opportunity for the Colonials to participate or give feedback. Government officials located in the capital cities of Spain and France made decisions for their colonies. Not only were decisions delayed as ships traveled back and forth to the

Spanish and French colonies, but the officials making these decisions had home-country political priorities which did not align with the needs of their colonies. Poor colonial management caused Spain to eventually lose its position as the dominant world power.

Britain hoped to obtain wealth from trading furs, and eventually profited from growing valuable crops in plantations in North America. Britain also saw that the settlers in developing colonies provided an export market for British goods, which increased British tax revenues. Britain had no extra funds to spare for administering the American colonies. It made economic sense for the British government to choose private British interests to operate and profit from colonial settlements. British leaders were not inclined to involve themselves directly in American colonial matters. The economic strength that Britain derived from its "hands-off" colonization later eroded the power of Spain and France. British colonies benefitted from self-management. American colonials used sound business practices and made good choices for themselves and their future.

Like Spain and France, the great distance to America prevented rapid communication from Britain to the Colonials. Letters and messengers transported in sailing ships took months to make the passage across the Atlantic Ocean, depending on the season and weather.

British officials avoided traveling to any of the American colonies. North America was a wild, uncomfortable place, and the amount of trade generated by each colony was small. The settlers who had arrived in America from Britain wanted a better, more prosperous life. In the beginning, large numbers died from starvation and disease. Over time, colonial settlers adapted to the unfamiliar environment in America and succeeded in creating a better life for themselves.

American colonial settlers were subjects of Britain and considered themselves to be British. The Colonials needed Britain's protection from attacks by native Americans. They also needed protection from aggression by other European powers. In addition to France and Spain, Sweden and Russia also sought to create their own colonies to profit from riches in North America.

Colonial political Assemblies were composed of the most able of the immigrants, making local laws and operating each colony. Each colonial Assembly made the key decisions for its colony. Each assembly grew more powerful as they grew economically.

British leaders appointed British aristocrats to become governors and judges in the colonies. Britain did not fund the salaries and expenses of these British-appointed officials. Instead, Britain required the Assemblies of each colony to pay the salaries of its British Governor, which saved the British government this expense.

The design of this political structure worked for the colonial settlers and their successive generations. The profits from trade obtained by local merchants gave them influence over the politics within each American colony. After operating the affairs of their own colonies over generations, these colonial Assemblies would not be agreeable to the political changes that Britain later sought to impose.

Colonial leaders controlled each Assembly's funds. The Assemblies learned to manipulate the British governors by withholding or distributing pay slowly to the Governors, to ensure that the Governors complied with the directions of the Assemblies. Colonial leaders maintained a high degree of control over these British-appointed Governors.

Colonial success may be related to the American personality traits of self-reliance and capacity for invention. Did the risky circumstances of settlement in North America force immigrants to adapt to survive? Or was it that the challenges and opportunities in the New World attracted people with self-reliant and inventive personalities? Either way, the colonies became more profitable.

The investors who founded the Southern colonies did so solely for profit. The Planters who first colonized the Southern colonies had already obtained experience from working in the Caribbean sugar colonies. These Caribbean colonies were brutal places to live and work, due to disease and extreme heat. The British, French and Dutch Planters in their Caribbean Island colonies profited by overworking and underfeeding a great number of African slaves transported there to grow and harvest sugar cane, then the most profitable crop in the world. Caribbean planters had no qualms about applying brutal tactics, terror, and torture to maintain control of their slaves. The Planters pushed their slaves to work hard in the hot, disease-ridden islands, resulting in a vast number of deaths of slaves.

The Planters later organized and operated their colonies in the Southern mainland strictly as businesses to maximize profits. They had no noble goals, such as obtaining religious freedom or creating a better way of living for all. Labor to operate the Southern colonies first came through transport of poor or disadvantaged people from Britain who agreed to become indentured servants for a set number of years to pay for their costs of transport, after which they were to receive a small amount of cash to enable them to improve their lives by being free to buy property or sharecrop for the few owners of the large plantations. Later, when it became more economical for the investors to use slaves from Africa, rather than indentured servants, the importation of slaves into the colonial plantations on the mainland increased dramatically. The number of large plantations multiplied, maximizing profits for investors and owners of the plantations.

Groups seeking religious freedom founded the Northern colonies. They sought to start new lives free from the strictures of European monarchs and established churches. Due to their gentle summer climate and longer winters, the Northern colonies were not suited for growing crops like tobacco. The northern Colonials were able to thrive in spite of the limitations of the Northern climate, due to the lack of warm weather diseases such as malaria, which had killed one in five immigrants in the Southern colonies. The Northern settlers shared common goals of freedom and a better quality of life. They worked together to better their communities for the common good, having a much greater percentage of people who owned property, and a much larger middle-class who took pride in their communities. Still, it took generations for all of the American colonies to grow in population and profitability.

Colonial economic success caught the attention of the leaders in Britain's Parliament. They were able to displace the Dutch colony of New Netherland as part of their plan to focus on colonization in the New World. As the American colonies were increasingly profitable, Parliament passed trade laws, seeking to share in colonial prosperity. Colonial merchants and planters ignored these trade laws. They had little fear of consequences for disobedience. It would have cost Britain more than it was worth to send British troops across the ocean to take measures to enforce tax collection. Even without the imposition of direct taxation on the colonies, the growth of British trade with America increased Britain's tax revenues collected from its citizens and corporations located in Britain, despite there being no direct taxes levied upon Colonials in America.

British-appointed Governors in the colonies complained to their leaders in London that the colonial Assemblies would not pay their salaries until the Governors complied with the Assemblies' directions. The British appointed Governors were typically chosen from Britain's Aristocratic families to serve in each colony for a limited period of time. Most colonial Governors expected to return to Britain at the end of their assignments. They did not enjoy life in the rough conditions in the Americas and were glad to return to Britain and undertake new assignments after their service as Governors. The revolving door of inexperienced British Governors coming and going allowed the elected Assemblies of each colony to dominate the new Governors when they arrived in America.

If Britain wanted to maintain a high degree of control over its colonies, Britain should never have granted extensive political and economic freedom to the settlers in America at the beginning of colonization. Placing the first Colonials in a situation where they had to "swim or sink" limited the British government's financial risk. But giving the Colonials control over their own affairs in the beginning made it difficult for Britain to assert control generations later. Although the colonials continued as British subjects, they had no political representatives in the British government. The lack of representation in Britain made no difference to the colonial Assemblies, which were satisfied with the extent of their local control, as long as they paid no taxes to Britain.

As the Colonials thrived, their success created incentives for other British settlers to relocate in America, for a chance to obtain prosperity. If they were willing to risk crossing the treacherous Atlantic Ocean, clear virgin land of trees, rocks, and plant crops, despite the risk of conflict with Native Americans, they could prosper. If they had remained in Britain, their chances for having a good life were lessened as the British Aristocracy assumed greater power within Britain, taking more land away from small landowners, and benefitting the rich to the prejudice of the working classes and the poor.

Each wave of new settlers had helped the American colonies to grow stronger. Long before the War of the Revolution ignited, British journalists and commentators predicted that the American colonies would become independent eventually.

As more settlers arrived, this increased demand for land. Descendants of the initial generations of settlers tended to move to the unsettled land in the west of the colonies, purchasing less expensive land as the east coast land became more expensive. It was much less expensive to live in the undeveloped West. Settlers had a greater burden to level trees and clear vegetation to make room to build homes and start farming. Conflicts arose with Native Americans as more settlers arrived and interfered with Native settlements.

Colonial purchases of goods from Britain increased each year. The increasing profits to British businesses raised tax revenues collected within Britain. At this same time, the American colonies shipped copious quantities of American goods into Britain. Orders for ships constructed by American shipbuilders cost one-half of the cost for the same ships in Britain. Trade was booming on both sides of the Atlantic Ocean. The British citizens in America and British citizens in Britain were all prospering.

The revenues raised from increased colonial trade allowed British leaders to purchase more ships and manufacture more weapons to help expand the reach of their British empire.

LESSON 3: *Underestimating the opposition's strengths is a common error in any conflict. Underestimation can be based on lack of knowledge, or more often, lack of perspective.*

As America's population grew dramatically, American colonial leaders gained more power to protect their economy and way of life. If the British leaders had understood the consequences of interfering with the colonial profits, the British could have tried a different approach to maximize the economic benefits derived from these colonies. By the beginning of the 1700s, seventy-five years before the war of the American Revolution finally ignited, Britain already lacked the power to dominate their American colonies.

The size of the population affected every nation's power and wealth. People, not machines, did all the work. More people meant more food, more goods, and more trade. Leaders of a nation with a larger population mustered more soldiers to fight with more weapons. By 1750, the rate of population growth in the American colonies was skyrocketing. In the 20 years between 1750 and 1770, the American colonial population increased about 80 percent, yet the British population only increased at a rate of 20 percent.

The chance for economic success continued to attract European settlers to America, from all parts of Britain, especially from the poorer areas of Scotland and Ireland. Before long, the American colonial population would be larger than the entire population of Britain. Preoccupied with the other problems their nation faced, the leaders in Britain did not appreciate the extent to which population growth had amplified American power.

LESSON 4: *Meeting problems early on, when they are smaller and usually less urgent, is the best course. When problems become urgent, they are more difficult to resolve.*

In the early 1700s, British commentators wrote letters and published essays highlighting the ramifications of the increasing American population. Burgeoning colonial trade created more jobs in Britain, where the government derived money from taxes on goods in Britain. American purchases of British manufactured goods and clothing also made large profits for British companies. In addition to funds generated by American trade, increased revenues came to Britain from their other colonies around the world.

At this time, the average American Colonial had more money, better opportunities for education, and better business opportunities than the opportunities available in Britain. Colonial Americans developed a sense of their "imminent greatness." British Prime Minister Sir Robert Walpole understood the benefits of the British/American trade. He rejected the attempts by other British politicians to increase British control, understanding the importance of freeing colonies from unneeded interference. After Walpole's 22 years as Prime Minister, his chosen political successors continued his sound economic policies for more than a decade, until younger, less insightful British leaders came to power in Britain's Parliament.

The four decades of Robert Walpole's political influence within Britain in the 1700s was a relatively peaceful time in Europe and a stable time in the American colonies. Walpole valued compromise. Under his leadership, Britain avoided unnecessary conflict with colonial leadership, collecting huge revenues from the growth of commerce and industry on both sides of the Atlantic.

A minority of the members in Parliament opposed Robert Walpole. These minority members had always wanted to impose British taxes on the American colonies. Walpole correctly assessed that imposing taxes on the American colonies would incite unnecessary trouble and interfere with trade. He focused on the importance of maintaining British security and stability. Even though British Governors in the American colonies had always complained that colonials refused to respect the Governors' authority. Walpole convinced the majority in Parliament to leave the American colonials alone.

To understand the American Revolution, it is important to understand the relationships of power between the British Prime Minister, the British Parliament, and the British King. During the 1600s, Europe and Britain went through tremendous turmoil until about 80 years before the American Revolution. Britain's Glorious Revolution took place in 1688, placing limits on the spending power of the British king and increasing the power of the British legislature known as Parliament. Before the Glorious Revolution, the British kings and queens had exercised unlimited power over Britain's foreign and military policy. The monarch at the time, be it a King or Queen, was the sole arbiter determining when to fight wars and how to spend the money of Britain, which resulted in wars taking place, in and out of Britain, without restraint.

The political changes from the Glorious Revolution limited the power of British monarchs. Parliament took over control over all spending by the British government, which increased Parliament's power to influence the Kings and Queens who came to power.

As a result, British Monarchs and Parliament were required to work together and reach an agreement on how to best spend money, including making agreements for spending relating to the British colonies which had been established around the world. The Monarchs and Parliament had to cooperate to be able to fund any war. Britain had become the most democratic country in the world at that time. The democratic capitalist British system of government enhanced British profits, which allowed Britain to become more

KING GEORGE III
(Image from the New York Public Library Collection)

powerful than Spain and France, whose monarchal bureaucracies and inefficiency weakened their economies. They lost trade to Britain, whose manufacturers made and sold better, less expensive goods than those made in either Spain or France.

In 1760, when King George III became King of Britain, the conflict with the American colonies had become intense. George's father died when George was age 12 but he did not take the British throne until age 21. It says something about George's personality that, in the first 11 years of George's reign, he changed prime ministers seven times.

Although George claimed that he acted for the good of his country, his good intentions paved the way for a poor result for Britain regarding America. He was a rigid thinker. He did not easily accept changing circumstances or novel ideas. Strongly believing in duty and obligation to his country, George would not tolerate disrespect to the British throne or Britain's Parliament.

In choosing only ministers who shared his own views, rather than choosing advisors like Robert Walpole, who would have given him honest advice, George isolated himself from arguments and ideas voiced by populist politicians. George was clearly in the camp of the wealthy Aristocrats. Insufficient consideration of the political arguments asserted by the populist opposition leaders prevented George from entertaining practical solutions which could have helped to avoid conflict with American colonial leaders and could have assisted the continued growth of trade with the American colonies.

Although George was highly intelligent, he had little experience. George did not understand how much he did not know. Despite his intellectual capacity, George never traveled to the continent of Europe, and never even traveled within Britain to the north of England. He could easily have traveled throughout the British Empire, but never did. George learned about America from reading books and newspapers. Other information came from advisors and government representatives returning from abroad, but they often filtered the information George received to serve their own interests and manipulations.

King George also struggled with mental health. In 1765, ten years before the Revolutionary War began, his ministers prevented George from seeing most of his own family members, although at the time, his illnesses were described as being physical in nature. The ministers protected George from disclosure of mental illness, as disclosure of the truth could have led to George's replacement.

Modern medical experts who have reviewed his writings agree that King George III was not suffering from the disease porphyria, which was the diagnosis given by physicians of his time. The consensus of modern physicians is that George suffered from bipolar mental illness. As early as 1765, when he was 27 years old, George appeared to have been suffering from episodes of mania and depression. His bipolar symptoms resolved in 1766, 10 years before America declared independence from Britain. King George would not have his next bipolar episode until 1785, two years after the Revolutionary War concluded.

Although he would frequently debate political problems with his ministers, George always acquiesced to their recommendations and advice. When something turned out badly, George felt satisfaction in saying, "I told you so…" to his ministers. The reality was that, even though he was King, George delegated decision-making to his ministers, despite his beliefs that his ministers were frequently wrong.

Moreover, King George's advisors were far from being the most talented and capable candidates to run the British government. Lord Halifax and Lord Townsend, two of George's chief ministers, were known to be heavy drinkers and gamblers. King George even admitted that Lords Halifax and Townsend were the worst men in England, yet he relied on their advice, probably because of their political influence in Parliament.

Parliament's quest to tax the American colonies was only one of the issues that concerned King George. There was turmoil in the convoluted politics of Britain, war with the French in Europe, and an expanding British Empire in India. George's main concern was that Britain exhibited strength. He would concede to solve a problem, as long as British authority was unchallenged and respected.

King George insisted that Britain never give in to the repeated colonial protests over British taxation. His rigid refusals to accommodate the Colonials provided zealous colonial radicals with arguments regarding Britain's bad intentions, which convinced more moderate colonials to support American independence. These radicals claimed that Britain wanted to enslave the colonials, and that Britain would never allow the thirteen colonies to prosper as they had in the past.

LESSON 5: *Obtain Reliable Sources of Information*

King George did not understand the importance of political leaders visiting their own domains and touring other nations first-hand. He did not meet or speak with people who lived outside the south of England. He failed to gather first-hand, reliable information about Britain's colonies around the world. His limited experience allowed his ministers' power to unduly influence his decision-making. If he had traveled to the 13 American colonies, George could have gained information first-hand to understand the colonial perspective, to evaluate Britain's best posture to retain the American colonies, and at the same time, maintain respect for British power. Instead, Britain's loss of the American colonies turned out to be George's greatest mistake.

King George was not alone in having limited knowledge of what was really happening in America. For the 15 years between the end of the war with the French in America in 1760 to the beginning of the Revolutionary War in 1775, no minister of the British government ever visited any of their trans-Atlantic colonies. Information sent from North America was second hand, often edited by political subordinates with personal agendas. Lacking first-hand knowledge, George and the leaders of Parliament were vulnerable to manipulation. They might have avoided mistakes if they possessed accurate information about the true state of affairs in the American colonies.

Visitors from the American colonies traveling to Britain observed the effects of political patronage, nepotism, deal-making, and corruption in the British government, which increased colonial concerns that there would never be fair treatment for Colonials. In contrast, foreign visitors coming to the American colonies from Europe were impressed by how the settlers in America had improved the quality of their lives, by taking advantage of the economic opportunities in the colonies.

British leaders came from the wealthy aristocratic class, consisting of about two hundred families, which owned a great percentage of the land in Britain. There was no way for other Britons to move into the aristocratic class. The medieval doctrine of Primogeniture had required the eldest sons to take over entire family estates in Britain, leaving the younger brothers of these two hundred families to find places in government to be able to support themselves. Younger sons of Aristocrats typically served in Parliament, wasting their time gambling, drinking, and womanizing, unconcerned with their political responsibilities.

Due to their own self-interest, members of Parliament who owned land in Ireland were vehemently against yielding to any colonial requests, fearing that more of their Irish tenants would give up farming in Ireland, and would emigrate to America, thereby depriving these British landlords of rents.

British leaders did not consider the value of accommodating colonial demands. The majority in Parliament assumed that most colonials would seek to remain British citizens no matter what. As the disputes over control of the colonies increased, Britain's influence over its citizens in America weakened.

Before Parliament passed laws to raise taxes on the American colonies, most British taxes came from import duties levied on merchants within Britain, as they imported products into Britain. Sneaking goods into Britain helped these merchants in Britain to avoid taxes and make more profits. Most merchants in Britain undertook substantial smuggling to increase their income. American merchants were also engaged in smuggling within the colonies to avoid taxes. It was comparatively easy to avoid taxes during these times, as it was difficult for governments to become aware of the extent of smuggling.

Britain's government collected taxes in Britain from the sale of sugar and molasses produced by slave labor in Britain's Caribbean sugar cane plantations. A by-product of making sugar, molasses was a base for manufacturing rum. Colonial merchants bought their Caribbean molasses, not from Britain, but from the French colonies, as the French were able to sell molasses at lower prices, due to their highly productive French slave colonies in the Caribbean. American smuggling and bribery of British tax officials regulating the rum trade was common.

Parliament's leaders had sought to make their British Caribbean colonies more profitable by passing the Molasses Act of 1733, which made it a crime for British subjects either in Britain or its Colonies to purchase less-expensive molasses from the French. Merchants must purchase the more expensive molasses produced by British Caribbean colonies or face criminal penalties. The sole purpose of the Molasses Act was to gain more money for the British government, at the expense of reducing the merchant's profits.

Merchants in Britain and merchants in the colonies protested and demanded a repeal of the Molasses Act. King George did not want to repeal this new tax, as Britain needed the money. If Britain did not obtain additional taxes from sales of molasses, George's only other choice was to raise taxes on other goods, which would increase the cost of other goods to British manufacturers and merchants, but American colonials would not contribute. The King, therefore, refused to ask Parliament to repeal the Molasses Tax.

SIR ROBERT WALPOLE
(Image from New York Public
Library Collection)

When the British government first attempted to prosecute tax evasion in America, colonial smugglers intimidated government witnesses who failed to appear in court. Colonial mobs threatened to destroy the homes of British tax collectors.

British Minister Robert Walpole, then still in power, rectified the conflict by failing to send British ships to police the trade, and refusing to enforce compliance with the Molasses tax. Lack of enforcement deflated the conflict. British merchants continued to smuggle.

Colonial merchants continued to buy molasses from the French colonies. Walpole defended his inaction, declaring that enforcement would require armed British forces to intercede with British merchants, risking violence within Britain. When asked to increase taxes solely upon the American colonies instead, Walpole stated: "I have Old England set against me, and do you think I will have New England likewise?"

LESSON 6: *Look for practical solutions.*

Robert Walpole was a flexible thinker. He looked for practical solutions, not bound by ideologies. Walpole balanced the needs of Parliament and the needs of the British merchants. He correctly foresaw that enforcement of tax collection would harm the economies in Britain and in America.

Robert Walpole understood that successful colonial trade had raised substantial tax revenues within Britain. The Colonials were spending their profits purchasing British-made goods. The benefits to Britain's merchants and the benefits to the British government from the sale of all British goods far outweighed the amount of money provided by enforcing the Molasses tax. Robert Walpole produced a "win-win" solution to this conflict, by not allowing Parliament's new law to interfere with the existing benefits of trade to Britain and to its American colonies.

More than a decade later, the election of new leaders in Parliament eclipsed Robert Walpole's influence. These young and aggressive politicians soon passed other tax laws aimed to help Britain share in colonial prosperity. These new leaders of Parliament were unconcerned with common-sense solutions. They passed laws imposing taxes upon the colonies with aggressive mechanisms in place for enforcement. Parliament's majority embraced the idea that Britain was the mother country and should demand obedience from its colonies. The new British leaders believed that they should treat American colonials like children, to obey Britain's leaders as they would obey their parents. Parliament knew that the prosperous Colonials could afford to pay more in taxes, so why not tax them?

LESSON 7: *People's expectations are important.*

British leaders did not see why Colonials would resist increased taxes. They did not consider that colonial merchants had ignored Britain's laws before. The Colonials had learned to avoid British taxes, due to lack of enforcement or due to repeal. The British government was unable to prevent British merchants from smuggling goods into Britain. The colonials in America, being British subjects, were aware of what their counterparts in Britain were doing. Why should Colonials pay taxes which were not paid by other British citizens?

Despite lacking any evidence that taxation of the American colonies would be successful, these new leaders in Parliament clung to their belief that Britain was in charge and could tax at will. This "battle of beliefs" would ignite the American Revolution years later, an outcome which the new leaders of Britain discounted as improbable. They grossly underestimated the power of the Colonials, and also overestimated their own ability to control events in America.

A neutral analysis of the situation by disinterested mediators could have provided Parliament with better information, and with practical alternatives to obtain the best result for Britain. If the leaders in Parliament could have seen this situation from the colonial perspective, Parliament's decisions would been more beneficial to Britain.

Most Colonials wanted to remain British citizens. Rebellion would have profound consequences. The British/American conflict was truly akin to a family dispute where a powerful parent attempts to control a willful adolescent. Instead of each engaging in dialogue and seeking to understand contrary opinions, when the parent applies force to offspring, one consequence may be rebellion.

LESSON 8: *Only apply force when absolutely necessary. During a conflict, applying force to the opposition, without adequately understanding the opposition's position, may produce negative consequences. When people will not concede in a negotiation because "they know that they will win," this may be overly optimistic, lacking good evidence to support their optimism. If one side states that they do not care about what happens if they lose, this is usually a weak negotiating posture, based upon emotional thinking, often lacking support in the facts of the situation. A very unpleasant surprise may await them, despite the confidence expressed in the prelude to fighting.*

After extensive time passed without enforcement, the British government instituted new taxes along with new mechanisms for aggressive enforcement, which aroused colonial protests. The new British leaders disregarded the objections of the Colonials. In short, the British decision-makers' belief that they could ignore colonial complaints, proved to be incorrect. The situation led to results which were worse for Britain, than if Parliament's leaders had merely continued to follow the practical advice of Robert Walpole, to leave well enough alone in the colonies.

Over the 20 years before the Revolution, Parliament passed more laws favoring Britain at the expense of the American colonies, but Britain had no ability to enforce them. The few times that enforcement took place, it cost more to administer than the value of the revenues obtained. More importantly, Britain's attempts to take a greater share of America's profits fueled the spread of revolutionary thinking in the colonies, due to the growing distrust of the motives of Britain's leaders.

LORD HALIFAX
(Image from the New York Public Library Collection)

Britain engaged in a series of wars in Europe, including a war against the French, later known as the Seven Years War. Naval battles took place on the open seas and in North America, where both Britain and France had colonies. The British believed that the French might attempt to conquer Britain's colonies in America, to usurp the benefits of trade with the Americans. Seeking to use the American colonies to defeat the French, British Lord Halifax arranged for a conference in America at Albany, New York, to meet with representatives of all the American colonies. Halifax's goal was to establish himself as the British "Commander in Chief" of the militias of the Colonies to fight the French. He also proposed to construct a series of British-controlled forts in the American colonies to enhance Britain's ability to defeat the French.

Lord Halifax disagreed with the foreign policy of former Prime Minister Robert Walpole which sought to maintain a balance of power in Europe. Halifax expressed that Britain's trade relationships with European allies were no longer of any use to Britain, that maintaining European relationships were expensive and unreliable. Under Halifax's influence, Parliament reduced trade with European allies, and focused on collecting greater profits from Britain's American colonies. Halifax did not anticipate that asserting greater control of the colonies would backfire, as colonial merchants used every means available to preserve their own prosperity.

At the Albany Conference, representatives from each of the thirteen colonial Assemblies advised Lord Halifax that none of them had the authority to bind their Assembly. The Assembly for each colony must ratify any agreement reached in Albany. Even if all the colonial Assemblies eventually approved, then Britain's Parliament must also approve. Not surprisingly, no agreement of any kind came out of the Albany Conference.

Colonial leader Benjamin Franklin defined the problem: the Colonies could only unite in a "voluntary union" rather than have a "union of colonies" forcefully imposed by Parliament. Franklin suggested that the Assemblies continue to govern within each colony, but a union of colonies might work, led by the British King and Parliament. Franklin understood that any union would have limited scope. He recognized that American colonial Assemblies would not accept control by British leaders. At the same time, British leaders would not allow a plan of union in any way limiting British power in America. The current "balance of power" between Britain and the Colonial leadership could not be upset. Even though a plan for mutual security and sharing of expense between Britain and the colonies was desirable, nothing could impair the existing powers of each.

British leaders suspected Franklin's motives were partisan. At that time in history, leaders of other nations often became involved in trying to help conflicting nations resolve their disputes, but a formal process of mediation using neutral mediators was not available.

Before meeting at Albany, Britain had dealt with each American colony individually, preferring to keep the colonies at odds with each other. Britain had avoided taking any step which might work to unify the colonies. Lord Halifax's Conference, however, joined the American colonies as a group for the first time, which laid the groundwork for colonial coordination going forward.

After the Albany Conference, a British commander arrived in America with orders to take control of the joint British and Colonial forces to fight against the French, but there had never been any formal agreement made. The colonial militias did agree to fight in coordination with the British troops. It was during these battles against the French that George Washington developed his skills as a General, which later helped him to achieve successes against British troops during the War of the Revolution. The war with the French also helped to train colonial fighters in the methods of British warfighting which would later strengthen the American Continental armies.

Historically, French settlers in North America had shown more consideration for Native Americans than the British. Always aiming to co-exist, the French chose not to displace Native Americans. Before this war, the French had established trading posts within Canada and the Great Lakes areas. They traded with the Native Americans without disturbing their way of life. Unlike the French, the British representatives did not seek to inhabit the same lands as the Native Americans inhabited. The British officials who came to America were aloof and disrespectful. They had no qualms about displacing Native Americans. Not surprisingly, when the war with the French started, the Native American leaders willingly fought with the French against the British troops and colonial militias.

During this time, British soldiers and sailors arrived in the American colonies to fight against Spanish troops, which had joined with the French as allies. The fighting between Britain and France took place in multiple venues, stretching all the way from the Philippine Islands in the Pacific Ocean to the islands of the Caribbean. Britain's

Parliament spent funds freely to create and support overwhelming military forces.

Due to Britain's need to provide food and supplies for British troops during this war, colonial merchants were able to charge the British exorbitant prices for supplies in the colonies. The British had no alternative. Colonial merchants emptied the pockets of the British as if they were a foreign power. Paying more for American goods to fight the French increased British expenses in North America and enriched colonial merchants.

No colonial-based British official wanted to report back home to superiors in Britain that the American colonial leaders had out-negotiated the British officials, making profits at Britain's expense. Instead, British officials in the colonies reported that Britain spent so much because the colonials were disorganized and unintelligent, unable to understand their own interests. British officials claimed that colonial fighters lacked courage, brains, adequate weaponry, and discipline as justification.

It is ironic that the war against the French created a financial bonanza for the American colonial merchants, as long as that war lasted. British currency flowed freely to supply British land and naval forces. Colonial privateers received cash commissions by Britain when they captured French ships. These privateers spent their British cash in the colonies.

Based upon reports of the Colonials' military inadequacies, Parliament's leaders believed that colonial fighters were incapable of achieving independence from Britain and that the Colonials could not be depended upon to fight, even when their own safety and well-being depended upon it. Parliament did not understand that the Colonials had successfully manipulated the British to pay more for supplies and to lead the fighting, lessening the risk of harm to colonial militias.

British troops and colonial militias eventually forced the French to withdraw from Canada. Having overspent to win the war with France, Parliament attempted to recoup a large part of its expenses by imposing additional new taxes upon the Colonials. Being the beneficiaries of increased security, Parliament believed that the Colonials should bear their share of the costs incurred to expel the French.

When the war against the French ended, the bonanza of British cash in the colonies ended. The post-war decrease in colonial profits hardened the Colonials' resistance to paying British taxes. The poorest Colonials had the most to lose. They had risked their lives in the war against the French, and now that the war was over, the Colonials had little money to purchase the necessities for living.

Colonial merchants' businesses were also struggling from the reduction in available cash following the war with the French. With a population of only one-third of France's population, Britain had defeated the French, primarily due to Britain's naval power. The Colonials remained British subjects following the war with the French. Moreover, despite the decrease in British cash after the war, the colonies remained prosperous. Unlike in Britain, there was no begging on the streets in the American colonies, and no starvation. Business was ongoing. Colonials were making their livings and were improving their homes and incomes. The threat of French attack receded. Britain's navy was far superior to any other navy in the world and would continue to protect its American colonies. Despite losing the war, the French continued to trade with the Colonials and remained in competition with Britain for this trade. Other European nations also sought to generate profits by trading with American colonies.

Colonials in America continued to buy British goods. French goods were more expensive and were not as good as those from Britain. Colonial merchants argued that the value of their trade to

Britain was high. From the colonial perspective, the profits to Britain from American purchases of British goods outweighed any need for colonial reimbursement to Britain for the costs of the war with the French.

Despite pressure from Britain, the Colonials objected to responsibility for British war debt. The British system of organizing armies was both expensive and inefficient. The American colonial fighters against the French had all been equal citizens, fighting together in militias, returning to their regular work when conflicts ended. The British system of obtaining soldiers was different: British high officers, usually aristocratic, undertook recruiting British soldiers in return for a money bounty from the British government for each soldier recruited to fight for Britain.

British military commissions and promotions of officers provided profits to the wealthy aristocrats. The British aristocracy paid to hire mercenary armies from other European countries. The British soldiers who actually served in the British armies included released debtors, pardoned criminals, paupers, and vagrants of questionable character. The Colonials looked down upon and refused to associate with the disreputable soldiers Britain had transported to fight against the French in the colonies. The Colonials refused to reimburse the British aristocracy for the exorbitant costs Britain had incurred in amassing their armies.

The Colonials believed that British leaders should treat Colonials with respect and concern, the same as British citizens in Britain. Driving the French out of America had assisted Britain with the balance of power in Europe, as well as in other parts of the world, another reason Colonials believed that Britain should bear the expenses of the war.

The end of the war with the French also accelerated colonial settlement into the American frontiers. In the 10 years between 1761 to 1771, the population of the State of New York grew from 80,000 people to 168,000 people. Achieving peace with the French had made relocation into the colonies more attractive to immigrants. The Native Americans were not happy with the aftermath of the war with the French. Although Britain had previously traded with Native Americans in the western lands and had supplied their needs, after the war with the French, the British reduced assistance to the Native Americans, using the money previously earmarked for Native American welfare to help pay for the war. At the same time, waves of settlers pushed the Native American tribes out of their lands, to the west.

At the end of the war with the French, the American colonies were only a few of the large number of European colonies already established throughout the world. The Caribbean, South America, Africa, and India were prizes that would increase trade and income for any European country with sufficient military strength to control those colonies. The most aggressive European colonizers at this time were Britain, France, and Spain. Each was looking for signs of weakness in other European countries. Most European nations would not hesitate to seize an existing colony from one another if the opportunity arose.

Massive immigration from Europe had fortified the American colonies. After Britain won the war with France, both nations made agreements to control different colonies around the world: The French ceded their North American colonies to Britain and withdrew French claim to any land between the Atlantic Ocean and the Mississippi River. As part of this same deal, the British leaders agreed to return to France three of the valuable Caribbean sugar islands which British troops had conquered during the war—Martinique, Guadeloupe, and St. Lucia. The French were also able to negotiate to retain fishing rights in parts of the Grand Banks of Newfoundland, even though Britain controlled Newfoundland. France also gave Britain uncontested control of France's colony of Senegal in Africa, along with four French Caribbean islands: Dominica, Grenada, St. Vincent, and Tobago.

In another part of this same deal, the French gave New Orleans and Louisiana to its ally Spain. The Spanish wanted to obtain control over the vast area of Louisiana as a buffer to prevent any attempt by Britain to conquer Mexico, then a colony of Spain. At the same time, the Spanish made a deal with the British, giving Florida to the British, with the British yielding back to Spain both Cuba and the Philippines in the Pacific. These European trades of colonies rapidly changed the playing field of world politics, on a scope that is unimaginable today. These major national changes are a good example of how the political world can change rapidly. Unexpected events can change peoples' circumstances in unforeseeable ways. The world is inherently unstable, requiring leaders to exercise caution in all political matters, as the current landscape may be reset unexpectedly.

The British settlement with the French gave Britain control of a much larger Empire, which spread British military power thin. Expansion made the British Empire more difficult to defend, and more difficult to govern. Britain's North American colonies and territories had tripled in size following these trades with France and Spain.

LESSON 9: *Just because you have been successful in the past does not mean that you will be successful in the future. Being able to adapt to changing circumstances is a key to achieving success.*

The dramatic political changes in the world at the end of the British war with the French demonstrate that the world is constantly subject to change. Most people do not adapt well to dramatic change. It is more comfortable to believe that the status quo will always be there, but that way of thinking leads to big mistakes. Unanticipated events frequently arise. It is important for leaders to accept the reality of change and navigate with open minds and flexible thinking, so as not to lose opportunities and advantages.

Experienced leaders expect changes. They have learned that major changes typically cause reverberations, triggering other changes. British leaders failed to recognize that population growth in the American colonies limited their options to try to control the American colonies. If the British had opened their minds to the idea that they could not prevent their American colonies from attaining independence, they could have planned for and created a gradual path for American independence, avoiding unnecessary conflict and maintaining America as a powerful ally of Britain. Instead, Britain's mercenary antagonism of its colonial citizens made war unavoidable.

Colonial merchants had learned to be practical as they solved the problems of making a living in the colonies. In the past, these merchants had never paid taxes from marketing their surplus flour, beef, and other products to people from any country who had the money to purchase them. Once the British anti-smuggling enforcement began, colonial smugglers aggressively intimidated prosecution witnesses who were set to testify against them. Mobs also threatened the homes of British tax collectors in the American colonies while these smuggling prosecutions were pending. New anti-smuggling laws imposed harsh penalties, but colonial merchants refused to accept the British enforcement and penalties.

The conflict ramped up when colonial leader James Otis wrote a pamphlet protesting a new British law requiring the Massachusetts colony to purchase, maintain, and staff a sloop ship with British soldiers for the protection of the ports of Massachusetts, and at the same time, Britain charged the Massachusetts colony for the expense of maintaining and staffing the sloop. Parliament unilaterally laid this expense upon Massachusetts without first having sought the approval of the Massachusetts Assembly. James Otis strongly criticized the British for abrogating the power of the Massachusetts colony, calling it "British Tyranny." One colonial commentator wrote at the time that it was better for Canada to have remained under French control, if the price for France's removal from America was that the British would undertake enslavement of the Colonials.

The perception of the British leaders was that the Assemblies of the American colonies had become too powerful and that Britain should be the decision-maker for the colonies. The majority leaders in Parliament had awakened to the increasing value of the American colonies. Collecting more taxes would help to finance the profligate lifestyles of Parliament's leaders. Colonials were frustrated that they had no representation in Britain. They had no ability to politically influence British leaders.

It made sense that Britain wanted to raise money from the American colonies to offset the British debts. But Britain was color-blind to the optics, which helped radical colonial revolutionaries convince mainstream Colonials that only a complete split from Britain would end Parliament's attempts to dominate and subjugate the American colonies.

Parliament responded by imposing a cider tax in Britain, which caused huge protests within Britain. British cider contained alcohol, so the new tax had the same effect as if the British government placed a new tax on beer. The political unrest generated from the cider tax forced repeal. British citizens showed their power to generate change in Parliament. American Colonials, unlike British subjects in England, had no power in Parliament. The refusal of British leaders to pay attention to colonial complaints reinforced the reality that Colonials were "second-class citizens" who would never have their own representation in Britain. More Colonials came to agree that only a complete split from Britain would solve this problem.

The members of Parliament pursued another opportunity: to profit from the sale of colonial land. King George had made friends with native American chiefs from unsettled territories who had visited Britain during the war with the French. Wanting to preserve the lucrative British trade in furs, and wanting to keep the chiefs happy, King George issued a new Proclamation in1763, making it illegal for the American colonials to buy land from the Native Americans in the territory west of the Allegheny Mountains. Parliament ratified the King's Royal Proclamation and directed that the region between the Allegheny Mountains and the Mississippi River was limited to Native American tribes, except that British and Colonial traders could remain in those territories if they purchased trade licenses from the British government.

Part of the motivation for the Royal Proclamation was that the British were afraid that colonial trade with native Americans could lead to more manufacturing of products taking place within the colonies, potentially reducing the profits from British manufacturers' trade with Native Americans. Moreover, the British economy and Britain itself might weaken from colonial competition if colonial manufacturing increased. Leaders in Parliament argued that the failure of Britain to undertake immediate control of colonial trade would result in the American colonies becoming much stronger and, therefore, more likely to seek independence.

The Colonials did not want to pay for licenses, to be able to continue to sell the goods they were already selling to the native Americans. The Royal Proclamation favored British speculators, to the prejudice of the Colonials who had already begun the process of investing in and exploiting the regions west of the Allegheny

Mountains. Colonial leaders believed that they had the greater right to dispossess the Native Americans, now that the French had departed.

Most British troops had returned to Britain after the conclusion of the war with the French, so there would be no military consequences to the Colonials if they ignored the Proclamation. British troops remained stationed in the coastal areas, far away from the lands between the Allegheny Mountains and the Mississippi River. British enforcement would require transporting a large number of additional British troops 3000 miles to America, and then marching these troops several hundred miles, crossing over the Allegheny Mountains into the wilderness of the American interior, while at the same time, maintaining sufficient supplies to feed and maintain the British troops, an undertaking which would have been very expensive, with doubtful chances of succeeding.

Not only did the Colonials fail to pay license fees or commissions, but Britain continued to maintain their own forts in the western lands. Keeping their forts did not increase British trade with the Native Americans. Unlicensed colonial traders continued to trade in the West, exploiting their established relationships with Native Americans. Britain was unable to enforce the Royal Proclamation.

Preoccupied with the need to preserve their sovereignty over the Colonials, British leaders never attempted to understand or accommodate the Colonials. Moreover, despite Britain's overall interest in maintaining good relationships with the Colonials, there was no mechanism for the British leaders positioned in the different departments of the British government to consult with each other, which prevented Britain from developing a comprehensive plan to deal with the American issues. A unified strategy could have helped Britain's relationship with the 13 colonies.

In the 10 years before the American Declaration of Independence officially started the Revolutionary War in 1776, the leaders on both sides of the Atlantic Ocean could see that war was becoming inevitable. Even so, the majority of colonials preferred to remain British subjects, if only life in America could return to the way it had always operated before the British attempted to take power away from colonial Assemblies.

Fanning the flames of the conflict were the radical American colonial political leaders, mostly merchants—who feared a loss of income from increased British taxation. These radical Colonials were the driving force for independence from Britain. However, most Colonials recognized the benefits of protection from Britain, the most powerful country in the world. The disputes could have ended if Britain had placed the Colonials on equal footing with the British citizens located within Britain.

Instead, Britain placed a stronger grip on the Colonials: Parliament voted to bring a greater number of British troops to the American colonies, both to protect from foreign invaders, and to quell protests of the Colonials. When more troops arrived, the Colonials did not back down. Just the opposite, the more control the British leaders attempted to assert, the more the conflict heated up.

Looking back and forward in history for a moment, in disputes around the world, equal and fair treatment of the local people has been shown to be the best antidote to colonial conflict. Failing that, total domination and extermination of local people who resisted control was often the method chosen by colonial powers to end local resistance. A colonizing power engaging in brutal repression is likely to face the great expense of supporting and maintaining remote military positions within a colony. The loss of lives of the soldiers of the colonizing forces from repeated revenge attacks by the colonial population usually offsets any financial benefits obtained from dominating colonies. Immigration to such repressed colonies was unattractive, as unrest causes newcomers to fear for their own safety.

In the decade before the Revolutionary war began, American colonial leaders proposed plans which would give Britain more control over trade, but otherwise would have allowed the colonies to govern themselves. The unintended benefit of the colonies drafting these proposed agreements with Britain was that the leaders of the colonies came into close contact with each other, as they coordinated to reach solutions which would satisfy Parliament. Colonials from different colonies had common interests and developed trust with each other. Close relationships developed among colonial leaders. These relationships helped to create plans for Revolution, after Parliament ignored colonial proposals.

LESSON 10: *Unfounded optimism regarding the outcome of conflict is known as "falling in love" with your position. It is unwise for leaders to think their position is so strong that nothing which the other side can do will harm them. Such situations are rare. Critical analysis helps to avoid mistakes. Each side needs to fully explore what could go wrong.*

One danger generated by unfounded optimism is that unforeseeable chance and luck may worsen one's position. Cautious leaders always plan for the potential downside, including the unexpected. If British leaders had addressed the American situation with open minds and understood the logic supporting the colonial mindset, negotiation would have provided an acceptable deal.

Instead, Britain took an obstinate path that led to exactly the opposite result that British leaders intended. Britain ended up fighting a war much more costly than the war with the French. At the same time, Britain compromised its valuable trade with the American colonies by applying force to obtain a greater share of the profits. The Germans have a wonderful word to describe a situation where a proposed "improvement" makes things worse: "Versichlimbesserung." There is no word for this concept in English, but that is exactly what happened when British leaders pursued a share of the Colonials' money. The war of the American Revolution severely drained British funds. This financial harm to Britain would not have happened if Parliament had accepted that their best outcome required satisfying colonial concerns.

As the conflict heated up, people in New York City rioted and destroyed the houses of British officers when the British attempted to enforce the Stamp Tax. Similar violence took place in other American colonies, until finally stamp distributors within the colonies closed shop.

This moment in history was the ideal time for Britain's leaders to have recognized their errors in thinking. Collecting taxes at the risk of destroying prosperous trade with the colonies was foolish. If British leaders had offered representation in Parliament or took other steps to assuage the colonials that colonial financial burdens in the future would be the same as in the past, there would have been no revolt. A return to the old relationship with Britain was all the relief which most Colonials sought. Parliament needed to calm and reassure the Colonials. Instead, King George and the leaders in Parliament insisted that the Colonials had no right to chart their own future.

Colonial leader Benjamin Franklin argued that British taxation of the American colonials had the effect of allowing one set of British subjects to exercise dominion over fellow British subjects, where there was no right to do so, that Parliament had unfairly usurped power over the British citizens inhabiting the colonies.

If King George had promised to make colonial taxation equivalent to the taxes paid by citizens in Britain, this would have stymied the colonial agitators for freedom. Colonial merchants would have been glad to see their businesses freed from the threat of unfair taxation. If

Parliament granted representation, giving Colonials a voice in Parliament, negotiation and compromise would have been much easier to attain.

The British leaders believed that it was in Britain's interest to hinder the growth of American colonial manufacturing: Not only were American manufacturers already in competition with British manufacturers, but large numbers of skilled British workers were relocating in America for higher wages and a better life. This exodus of British workers threatened to reduce the British population at the same time that the American population was expanding. Political agitator Samuel Adams wrote in the colonial newspapers that it was absurd for a distant government in Britain to control events in the American colonies, especially when the population of the American colonies would soon eclipse the population in Britain.

In response to Parliament levying more taxes upon Colonials, New York merchants threatened to stop doing business with Britain. The merchants voiced that they would be in no hurry to pay past debts to

English merchants and banks. After giving notice to the British, the leaders of all of the American colonies agreed to stop ordering goods from Britain, which began a non-importation policy against Britain. The resulting decline in demand for British goods from America put British laborers out of work. Wages in Britain fell due to competition for the few jobs which were available. Prices for food and housing rose in Britain. The common people of Britain suffered. Political pressure within Britain demanded that Britain's leaders do something to fix the situation.

This colonial non-importation tactic had an additional benefit for colonial merchants: British goods already imported to the colonies soon became scarce, increasing demand, which allowed colonial merchants to raise prices for those British goods already in their warehouses. The colonial merchants made greater profits, although people in the colonies had to pay more for these goods.

George Washington and Benjamin Franklin agreed with the strategy of non-importation. Britain lost business and jobs as American colonial orders for British goods evaporated. British merchants and British laborers felt the sting as their businesses slowed down. There were other benefits for the Colonials: They were no longer spending money in Britain, which reduced overall debt from the Colonials to Britain. The higher cost of British goods also encouraged Colonials to build their own factories in America, increasing production of the same types of goods manufactured in Britain. The benefits from reduced spending and development of colonial manufacturing outweighed the harm to the colonies from the loss of trade with Britain.

Within 1 year after undertaking the non-importation policy, American exports to Britain decreased by 40 percent. Large numbers of British workers lost their jobs, because non-importation had created a surplus of goods within Britain, which also drove down the prices for in goods in Britain. The British people could now buy British-made goods within Britain for less than those goods cost to produce. Manufacturers within Britain stopped manufacturing and laid off their workers until all the previously manufactured goods were sold off.

Large British manufacturers failed because their overhead expenses did not disappear when colonial purchases stopped. In contrast, most colonial manufacturers had smaller overheads, and were able to adapt to reductions in sales. The decline of British business caused a loss of tax receipts for the British government. Reduction of tax receipts and job losses ignited a political storm within Britain, which soon led to Parliament repealing the new taxes on the American colonies. Non-importation proved that the colonies had the power to force Britain to make changes.

But, one-by-one, the American colonies gradually opened up British trade again, due to local political pressure from those colonial merchants whose businesses had suffered most from the stoppage of trade. The end of non-importation by individual colonies highlighted the need for the colonies to act in unison to exert maximum influence upon British leaders.

LESSON 12: *Name-calling inflames emotions and displaces rational problem-solving. Attempting to inflame emotion, claiming that the other side is "bad, is a counter-productive tactic, whose purpose is to trigger negative emotions, so that people will close their minds to rational opposition arguments. This tactic often prevents reaching a settlement.*

Members of Parliament made incendiary statements to the British public that the conflicts with the colonies were based solely upon an unjust American quest for independence from Britain. Yet the reality was that most colonial people wanted to remain under British protection, provided that British leaders would stop trying to impose unfair taxes.

British leaders characterized the Americans as being greedy and ungrateful. These statements obfuscated Parliament's prior missteps in handling colonial matters. It was convenient and expedient for Parliament's leaders to wrongly claim that the Colonials' goals were unreasonable and unjustifiable.

More problems arose when Britain imposed new legal procedures for the American colonies, which allowed British officials to obtain search warrants called "Writs of Assistance." A British Customs official, armed with one of these Writs, could search colonial premises to look for evidence of smuggling. In response, colonial merchants organized behind the scenes, to convince the colonials of the need for revolution, due to Britain abrogating the rights of British subjects located in the American colonies.

LESSON 13: *The Benefits of Being Reasonable*

Mediators often hear the following comment at failed mediations: "The other side's position was so extreme that they made it easy for me not to settle. If they had been more reasonable, I would have worked harder to find a solution. But now, since the other side is acting unreasonably, nobody will blame me for not settling. Others will not criticize me for not reaching a settlement, even if the end result of conflict goes badly for our side."

As the majority leaders in Parliament created new laws, aiming to extract monies from the American colonies, the minority in Parliament argued that it was useless, impossible, and costly to try to control the American colonies. The minority leaders argued that forcing the

Colonials to pay taxes to Britain would cost far more than any benefit which Britain could gain.

If Britain had merely promised not to impose taxation going forward, this would have prevented the imminent rebellion. The majority of British leaders in Parliament felt that abandoning taxation of the colonies would only delay resolving the situation to a time when the colonies would be even more self-sufficient. Parliament's majority believed that Britain must assert control of the colonies now or give up trying. They could not agree to a middle ground with shared power and control in the colonies. The majority in Parliament were over-confident that colonial leaders would eventually recognize obligations of duty and obedience to Britain and would eventually comply with paying British taxes.

The minority in Parliament, together with a number of political commentators in Britain, voiced that the American Colonials should have equality with other British citizens. They argued that the British had been making laws solely for the advantage of Britain, to the prejudice of British subjects in the American colonies. These British journalists and politicians wrote that the best course for Britain was to give up control of the American colonies and retain a good relationship going forward, based upon friendly terms. Parliament's leaders rejected these arguments.

More American Colonials agreed that it was impossible for negotiation with British leaders to create a better outcome, due to Parliament's unyielding stance. As choosing revolution became more popular, colonial wives pressured their husbands to join the patriot cause.

It is important to note the extent of dissent in Britain as well as the dissent in the American colonies. On both sides of the Atlantic, voices for war drove the conflict to war. Britain's unwillingness to compromise gave ammunition to the colonial revolutionaries. If citizens on both sides of the Atlantic had better information, their voices could have helped avoid war. But the British leaders and the American merchants were both convinced that war was the best alternative.

Conservative colonial leaders wanted to compromise with Britain, to try to remain under British protection, as British citizens. They asked King George to recognize that the colonial Assemblies were to the colonies what the Parliament was to Britain. Colonial leaders argued that the King should petition the colonial Assemblies for money if the King felt the colonies owed money to Britain. These colonial leaders spoke out against the unfair application of power by Parliament, but they did not dispute the power of the King, and of the British Empire.

Benjamin Franklin had continued to look for a solution to the conflict. He asserted that the leaders for both sides recognized the impropriety of the manner in which the new taxes were imposed. Yet Franklin argued that the colonies should pay British taxes, and that the colonies should admit that Parliament had the right to impose tax duties. Franklin understood the need for "give and take" to help achieve a settlement. The British leaders' main concern was to avoid showing weakness and to maintain Britain's status among the other nations.

The Colonials would not accept second-class treatment. Parliament refused to grant the Colonials the same political support as other British citizens because colonial participation in Parliament would dilute the political power of Britain's current leaders. If colonial representatives had a seat at the tables of power in Britain, what would happen as America's population continued to increase? Would the Colonials eventually have the majority in Parliament and control the operation of all of the British Empire?

Parliament's majority leaders regarded the Colonials as outsiders who had no place in the British social system. Parliament lacked sufficient information about colonial motivations to be able to make better choices. Had the British leaders been able to keep open minds, and had they agreed to sit down at a table with American colonial leaders, with the aid of mediators, it is much more likely that faulty British assumptions about the Colonials could have been dispelled, and some sort of agreement would have been reached to avoid the impending war. It was possible to create a forward-thinking solution that would have satisfied both sides, being aware that America's power would continue to increase.

Instead, British leaders sent six hundred British troops to Boston, the city experiencing the most political unrest. Not surprisingly, the citizens of Boston resented the presence of British soldiers. After these British troops arrived in March of 1770, a dispute arose, which led to a colonial mob attacking a British sentry, the melee leading to the deaths of five Colonials and nine British troops. The Colonials referred to this event as the "Boston Massacre." After this unfortunate incident, British leaders notified the Governor of Boston that any person charged with the crime of treason against Britain would stand trial in Britain, instead of standing trial before a jury of Colonials.

This British legal maneuver violated the established rights of all British citizens, long accustomed to trials with juries composed of their peers. British disregard of the Colonials' civil rights to trial before a jury of other Colonials gave weight to the accusations of the radical pro-revolutionaries that Britain's goal was to subjugate the Colonials, to treat them as "second-class citizens," denied of the rights enjoyed by citizens in Britain.

Parliament's leaders then made what they thought was a brilliant decision to tax tea being sold to Colonials because tea was one of the few items sourced outside Britain, so that an American boycott regarding the tea would have no effect in Britain. The British East India Company had purchased an excess amount of tea, which was inexpensive, and Parliament saw an opportunity to profit. British leaders believed that Colonials would rush to buy this tea, which was still less expensive than the tea sold by colonial merchants, even with the added tax. Tea was an important commodity in the colonies, which no colonial household could do without.

Parliament did not anticipate the response of the Boston merchants, who saw that cheap tea from Britain would reduce their profits. These Boston merchants organized a protest of dock workers and sailors and supplied them with free liquor and food. As the day of protest progressed, intoxicated protesters rioted and destroyed the homes of two wealthy colonial officials in Boston, whom the rioters portrayed as corrupt and pro-British. These tea protests in Boston spread to other colonies, where colonial tax collectors' homes were damaged and destroyed by vandalism.

Colonial merchants in Boston next convinced a group of dock workers and boatmen to destroy the forty-five tons of the British tea contained in 342 wooden chests, located on the British ships in Boston Harbor. This group of laborers masqueraded as Native Americans, boarded the British ships, and then tossed all of the chests of tea into Boston Harbor, ruining the tea. This extreme vandalism appalled the British. Colonials of the middle classes and upper classes also complained that such actions were inappropriate. The well-off Colonials understood how unlawful plundering harmed the relationship with Britain. It makes sense that financially well-off citizens saw no benefit to joining with lower-class agitators to incite rebellion against a current government, in favor of forming a new government. Prosperous Colonials were afraid of violent mobs in the streets. American colonial radicals, agitating for revolution, did not care about wealthy Colonials. The radicals believed that the wealthy Colonials were too supportive and too compliant with British power.

In response to the Tea Party vandalism, Britain sent ships to shut down the Port of Boston. Their plan was to strangle business in Boston, as fishing, commerce, and most occupations in Boston must come to a halt when colonial ships were unable to leave Boston Harbor. British leaders believed that closing Boston Harbor would break colonial resistance. They assumed that the other American colonies would not support the law-breaking undertaken within the Massachusetts colony. Closure of Boston's port, however, achieved the opposite: other American colonies joined together to come to Boston's aid. When British officials tried to hire colonial carpenters to build barracks for British troops in the Boston vicinity, no Colonial would agree to do this work.

Due to the ongoing conflict, Boston's official government ceased to exist. At the same time, Massachusetts radicals were manufacturing and storing weapons for later use against the British. These conflicts and controversies hardened the British stance. Both sides became inflexible, even though most Colonials thought of themselves as British citizens and wanted to remain British. They did not want to fight against Britain's powerful military, but more Colonials began supporting independence as the safer choice, as the colonial radical agitators for freedom were likely to destroy the property of any colonial perceived as cooperating with the British.

Britain's blunders in Boston fueled the rebellion. Any Colonial advocating in favor of letting the British have their way risked retribution by radical colonials. The strategy of the radical colonial agitators to bring on the war was working. Jurors refused to participate in trials. Colonial resentment boiled over. The majority leaders in Parliament became concerned that the British loss of the American colonies might motivate France and Spain to join to attack Britain, to gain control of Britain and the British colonies around the world.

Leaders from the thirteen colonies met at the Continental Congress of 1774, the first collaboration of all thirteen colonies to act in their common interest. Although under British law, it was illegal to meet to discuss rebellion, there was nothing that Britain's Parliament could do to stop the Continental Congress from taking place. Moderate colonials who wanted to remain British subjects were powerless to stop representatives from the thirteen colonies from meeting. Britain had not anticipated that the colonies could create a unified organization. Moderate colonials would have preferred to create their own coalition with the colonial loyalists to avoid war and to remain part of the British Empire. But the moderates knew it would be dangerous to argue against revolution when the colonial lower classes might use mob violence against anyone who argued against revolution. The people at the bottom of the colonial economic order were not prosperous. They were eager to create dramatic changes in their government, which might benefit them. The families of British sympathizers and British officials who lived in the American colonies were at the mercy of rebellious colonial mobs. British officials began resigning from their positions, returning to Britain out of fear.

The formation of the Continental Congress began a colonial "shadow government." The leaders from the colonies who attended the Continental Congress created committees which answered solely to the Continental Congress, not to the colonial Assemblies. During the Congress, the delegates were unable to reach agreement. Most agreed that achieving complete independence required waging war with Britain. The majority at the Congress refused to go along with any form of conciliation with the British.

The more conservative representatives at the Congress were able to persuade the other representatives to draft and send to the British King a letter, later known as "The Olive Branch Petition," seeking reconciliation with Britain, if Britain agreed to expand the rights of the

Colonials. In response, King George issued a proclamation declaring the Colonials to be in rebellion, which only inflamed the situation.

Colonial leaders at the Continental Congress then drafted and sent a second letter to British General Thomas Gage, then commander of all British troops in the American colonies, threatening that war was likely if Britain continued to infringe upon rights to self-governance that had existed since the founding of the colonies. After receiving this letter, General Gage did not take any action which might agitate the Colonials. He knew that he had too few troops to win in a battle with the Massachusetts colonial militia. Colonial militias would overwhelm British troops if rebellion took place before reinforcements arrived. Gage was pessimistic about the British chances to succeed in a war at that time. He suggested to leaders in Britain that they suspend the newly imposed taxes. He received no response.

Before the fighting started, the Continental Congress wrote to British newspapers, warning British citizens of over-reaching by the British government, and denying that the Colonials were seeking independence from Britain. These letters stated that all the Colonials wanted was a return to the status quo as it had been after the war with the French, restoring the harmony between Britain and the Colonials. This letter had no effect, as the British public had already become convinced that the Colonials were despicable people who needed to learn to behave.

Parliament then ordered General Gage to arrest the colonial leaders and their assistants. Although Gage had previously requested that Parliament provide 20,000 more British troops, no additional troops had arrived. Not having enough soldiers to be sure of winning battles, General Gage delayed moving against colonial leaders. When General Gage finally ordered his British troops to arrest colonial leaders, the British faced fierce opposition from colonial soldiers willing to die to obtain freedom from British rule. General Gage found himself in a difficult spot. He had only 5,000 men to protect all of the British interests in the 13 American Colonies.

Moreover, Gage had been living in the American colonies, on and off, for more than 20 years. He was married to a colonial woman and was well-liked by the American colonial leaders. Benjamin Franklin judged Gage to be "a cool, prudent man." Eight years later, after the settlement of the Revolutionary War, Gage confessed that, despite his close connections in the colonies, he had not foreseen the impending revolt.

LESSON 14: *Regular reassessment of conflicts is desirable to ascertain settlement opportunities.*

If British leaders had paid attention to the warning signs of the impending revolt, they might have been able to change their position and retain the American colonies. Even if they had been able to offer acceptable terms to the Colonials, however, the conflict may have gone too far gone too far by then to be able to make an agreement. By this point, it could have been political suicide for the majority in Parliament to make an abrupt about-face and give the Colonials what they had asked for earlier. The British public had already been convinced by British leaders' prior speeches that the Colonials were undeserving. British leaders believed it was important to project that Britain was strongly opposing the unreasonable and selfish Colonials. Giving in to colonial demands at this late time would have shown weakness on the part of Parliament.

The anti-monarchal British radical revolutionary Samuel Adams published pamphlets arguing that the past generation of British leaders had shown wisdom and valor, which allowed them to grow rich and powerful. But the descendants of the past leaders had fallen into pursuit of luxury and dissipation, to satisfy their own vanity and extravagance by grasping towards the honest earnings of industrious British emigrants in the American colonies. Samual Adams argued that the unwise actions of the British leaders deserved mistrust and hatred, that the Colonials must dissolve every connection with Britain. He claimed that the British needed the American Colonials more than the Colonials needed them.

British leaders delayed fighting against Colonials, to make sure that the British armies would win every battle through use of overwhelming numbers of troops. Although British ships had demonstrated sufficient power to close Boston Harbor, Britain had not yet sent enough troops to overwhelm the Colonials in a land battle. Two years later, in 1776, additional British troops finally reached the colonies. This two-year delay gave the Colonials more time to prepare for war.

At that time in history, Britain controlled the most powerful military in the world. Anticipating a difficult struggle, colonial leaders acted to arm every male in every household of the colonies. Increased organization and training of colonial militias took place throughout the American colonies leading up to the war.

The Continental Congress elected George Washington to lead the Continental Army. To become part of an effective army, his troops had to yield their own freedom and blindly obey the orders of their Continental commanders. The temporary sacrifice of their personal freedom was necessary to obtain long-term freedom from British control.

Colonial loyalists argued that the disruption of the relationship with Britain and mob violence were greater threats to freedom than paying taxes to the British. The loyalists feared descent into anarchy and civil war. British oversight had helped to maintain law and order.

The loyalists felt that the revolutionaries were creating false hope in the lower classes that revolution would help to raise the lower classes from the bottom of the economic order. The radical colonials had no regard for the authority of the British or the authority of the well-to-do Colonials and loyalists.

THOMAS PAINE
(Image from the New York
Public Library Collection)

Thomas Paine's pamphlet *Common Sense* appealed to ordinary people in the colonies. Paine explained how the British were acting against colonial interests, and why revolution was inevitable. Colonial loyalists saw Thomas Paine as a cracked-brain zealot and adventurer, whose ideas were dangerous. Thomas Paine's straight-forward ideas spread, easily repeated, until the majority of Colonials agreed that revolution was the only choice.

Thomas Paine argued for a more rational and decent ordering of societies throughout the world, which could only be achieved by rebellion. He argued against the hereditary rule by monarchs on the basis that rule by imbecile offspring of a former king or queen put nations at risk.

Additional Paine articles, published anonymously, denounced the slave trade. Paine implored colonials to see themselves, not as citizens of a particular colony, but as Americans. His argument that Britain's leaders wanted to make the Colonials into slaves demanded action for independence.

Most important, Paine argued in favor of creating a multi-ethnic, religiously free country. He argued for separation from Britain immediately, as separation from Britain would have to come eventually. He claimed that it would be easy for America to build an army and navy. Why should a much smaller island nation from far away rule this huge continent? Paine suggested that war with Britain would be short, victory for the colonies assured.

Once the Revolutionary War was in progress, Paine continued to write motivational pamphlets, urging the Colonials to keep fighting. His rousing encouragements, including the one that began: "These are the times that try men's souls," had the effect of encouraging more young men to enlist in the Continental Army. He wrote such lines as "If there must be trouble, let it be in my day, that my child may have peace." He suggested that Britain's mercenary Hessian soldiers would assault and rape colonial women. Thomas Paine's incendiary writings strengthened the resolve of Colonials to fight and keep fighting.

Paine's later writings and actions reveal that he believed that the concept of monarchy itself was an outdated, evil form of government. He wrote that organized religions were bad, but he kept these writings in the background during the war. Decades later, Thomas Paine also participated in the overthrow of French monarchy in that revolution.

Paine abhorred the power of wealthy merchants, despite the merchants favoring colonial independence. After the American Revolution was successful, Thomas Paine harmed his own reputation by attacking George Washington's integrity for having improperly profited from his political position. Washington had earned tremendous celebrity from his success in defeating the British armies. Thomas Paine could not maintain his relationships with the American leaders after the Revolutionary War ended. Attacking the integrity of the new American government officials had made him very unpopular.

Thomas Paine's thinking was visionary: he defined the modern role of governments, envisioning direct action by government to alleviate the suffering of the poor and providing financial safety nets. His writings continue to influence politics today.

Benjamin Franklin had been a strong voice in favor of negotiation with Britain, but his experiences while spending time in Britain convinced him that the British government was rife with corruption. As war approached, Franklin concluded that the colonies would be better off without any ties to Britain. It was better to risk death, rather than live lives as second-class British citizens.

LESSON 15: *Pay close attention to reasonable arguments from all sides.*

Before war erupted, Edmund Burke, a very sensible and practical British politician sitting in the minority party of Britain's Parliament, gave speeches attempting to convince the majority in Parliament to pacify the American colonies as much as possible to keep them in the British Empire. Parliament's majority believed that the best course was to enforce obedience by the colonies. Majority leaders assumed that the Colonials must fear to face a powerful British army, that the Colonials lacked the necessary qualities to be good soldiers.

Edmond Burke echoed the arguments of Robert Walpole from decades before, that the American Colonies had found prosperity due to a "wise and salutary neglect" by Britain. Burke argued against applying force to the Colonials. He pointed out how the destructive use of force was contrary to the relationship Britain should seek to preserve. Burke acknowledged that, in the past, no one in Britain had foreseen that the American colonies could be sufficiently united so as to rule themselves, but a new American government had arisen, with the Continental Congress, providing order. Burke argued in favor of making concessions to the Colonials, stating that "The retention of America was worth far more to the mother country economically, politically and even morally, than any sum which might be raised by taxation, or even than any principle so-called of the (British) Constitution."

Burke suggested that a "give-and-take," compromise and barter, could balance the struggle between the two sides. He suggested that freedom itself was the best way to bind the Colonies to Britain, to help secure the wealth of the world for Britain.

Britain's Parliament voted down Burke's proposal for settlement with the American colonials by a count of 270 against 78 on the basis that giving in to the demands of American Colonials would decrease the use and value of these colonies. The majority was optimistic that the Colonials would quickly yield to combined economic and military pressure from Britain.

Both the British and the Colonials assumed that fighting was better than settling. The British would have made better decisions if they had a more accurate picture of the true circumstances in the colonies. The Colonials might have made better decisions if they anticipated how fighting the war could create tremendous problems for the colonies, win or lose.

In February of 1776, Britain declared that all colonial ships were subject to seizure as property of open enemies. The British also hired mercenary Hessian troops from Germany to fight against the Colonials. These bold British actions forced Colonials to fight a war for independence. Most agreed that there was no longer any chance to stop the war.

Parliament's leaders failed to demonstrate that they did not wish to enslave the Colonials, that they had no malicious intent. To deflate the colonial rhetoric, Parliament could have yielded to the Colonials on at least one or two issues. If the British leaders had conceded the validity of any of the colonial protests, this might have quenched the revolutionary urge. However, the majority in Parliament maintained their unyielding stance, believing that the Colonials would never take the chance to fight a war for independence. Even if a war started, the Colonials had no chance of victory.

Even at this late time, representatives of Parliament could have met with and reached a deal with the colonial leaders. A deal would not please the politicians in Britain, but reaching an agreement would preserve the valuable trading relationship. The British leaders wanted revenues from collecting taxes, yet the risk of losses from the destruction of trade between Britain and the colonies was magnitudes larger than any funds which could be raised through taxation.

Finally, Parliament insisted that General Gage initiate fighting. While waiting for more troops to arrive, Gage sent troops to Lexington and Concord, Massachusetts. This battle resulted in casualties for both sides, and most importantly, the fighting provoked colonial resistance on a massive scale. Three days after signing the Declaration of Independence on July 9, 1776, a colonial mob toppled the Statue of King George and melted it down to provide lead for the manufacture of colonial ammunition.

Both sides of this conflict suffered casualties and wasted money fighting. The war risked exposing both Britain and the American Colonies to attacks from other colonizing nations. The rebelling Americans had chosen a difficult path, but at least they were acting in their own self-interest. The British had acted strongly against their own interests, and later regretted proceeding to war.

Colonial leaders did not want to upset American colonial society, or to change existing traditions, or to change the way the colonies operated in any dramatic way. Even if the Colonials were successful in their efforts to separate from Britain, the Americans would need to create a governmental structure to unite the colonies, yet at the same time, preserve the power of the colonial Assemblies. After 8 years of fighting to gain independence from Britain, more than a decade afterward, the 13 United States finally agreed to terms cementing a new Union of the American States.

LESSON 16: *A mediator can only do so much. It is effective to have a neutral mediator explain, "No, the other side is not being silly or irrational; they do have valid concerns. We need to address your concerns and their concerns and see if we all can reach a settlement addressing everyone's concerns which will avoid future conflict and preserve a happy relationship."*

The hawkish representatives of Britain and the radical revolutionaries in America were glad to fan the flames of conflict, each believing that fighting the war would result in their best outcome. Parliament needed to be willing to hear the truth, to finally understand that war was futile, that Britain would not be able to force the Colonials to provide tax revenues to Britain.

Leaders of powerful nations who have succeeded before often believe that they cannot lose going forward. Having won battles before, such leaders stop looking closely at the opposition and stop analyzing the circumstances where they find themselves. These leaders embrace unfounded, overly optimistic assumptions about what the future will bring, even though experienced leaders should be aware that bad luck and unforeseen events frequently happen, bringing unwanted consequences, even to the powerful.

This is why it is important for opponents to sit down and discuss issues with a mediator who can question, "Why do you assume that?" Candid discussion may raise awareness of potential negative consequences. A mediator might have helped to inform British leaders that their assumptions about the future might be without basis.

One of Britain's vulnerabilities was that the British Empire had grown beyond what the British military could protect. In 1775, the total number of sailors in the British navy everywhere in the world was only 18,000. At the same time, the British had not maintained sufficient funds to keep their military vessels in good repair, nor did Britain have sufficient funds to purchase adequate supplies. Britain was unprepared to fight a war against the Colonials.

British leaders relied upon Colonials wanting to remain British subjects, believing that only a small minority of Colonials wanted independence. The British also assumed that loyalists would fight alongside the British military against colonial rebels.

The Colonials knew what they were fighting against, but they still had to figure out what they wanted to be going forward. Would they have a king? Would they form a republic or other government? What would be the effect of separation from Britain? Would Britain continue to be a great power?

In July of 1776, British Commander-in-Chief William Howe finally arrived in New York with a huge military force of 32,000 experienced troops, far outnumbering the less experienced troops that General Washington mustered in the Continental Army. The British troops included 8,000 Hessian mercenary fighters from Germany. Washington commanded a total of 19,000 Continental troops. Although the British counted on support from loyalists in New York, colonial mobs assaulted and paraded loyalists through the streets. The mobs tortured loyalists by stripping them naked and burning them with candles. The mobs quickly drove most loyalists into hiding.

British General Howe initially won a victory over the American Continental troops on Long Island, New York, causing four times the number of casualties to the Americans as the British had suffered. After his victory on Long Island, General Howe did not aggressively pursue American General George Washington's army. If Howe's massive army had chased down and defeated Washington and his troops before they departed Long Island, the war might have ended then.

General Howe did not pursue Washington's army as Howe wanted to preserve the lives of his own troops by offering a deal to the Americans with regard to future taxes and pardoning colonials who surrendered. But General Howe did not have the authority from Parliament to make specific promises regarding terms with which Parliament could agree. When presented with Howe's personal proposal, the American leaders felt that there was no real choice but to continue to fight the war.

LESSON 17: *The power of both sides to make decisions is a prerequisite to achieving a settlement. It is fruitless to try to settle a dispute when there is insufficient authority to reach an agreement.*

Today, with instant communications universally available, it is easy for the decision-makers to participate during negotiations. But in 1776, colonial leaders perceived that Parliament was unlikely to agree to any settlement, simply because of the passage of time needed to transmit the proposed settlement terms to Britain. How could the fighting stop, given Parliament's refusals to make any earlier concessions to the American Colonials? General Howe was not in a position to make any valid settlement offers. Howe had not obtained Parliament's agreement for settlement terms prior to Howe and his troops departing from Britain to America.

Distance disadvantaged Britain: It took two to three months for communications and planning to pass back and forth between the British military in the American colonies and the British leaders in London. Moreover, British generals and their armies needed to coordinate. Often the battle plans sent from London were outdated. Coordination between the British armies was difficult, especially due to the geographic span of the colonies. British generals traveled back and forth to London during the war, creating delays and miscommunication. In contrast, the local knowledge of the American militias allowed them to operate independently, to improvise, to solve problems, while the British armies in America were idle, awaiting further orders from Britain.

British leaders in London did not want to make a deal which the Colonials could live with, and the Colonials knew this. Once the war started, there was no viable opportunity to negotiate until the Colonials proved that British success was impossible. The British were unwilling to negotiate until they finally came to understand that there would be no victory, that the war would continue indefinitely.

After the war started, General George Washington ordered the execution of Colonials selling goods and provisions to the British in Philadelphia. He also ordered his army to take provisions from the local farms, to avoid starving his troops. Taking their food did not endear General Washington to the colonial population of Pennsylvania. As the Continental government had no ability to tax, each state had to pay its own Continental troops, but payments were often late. Failure to pay sometimes resulted in mutinies of Continental troops which, when put down, resulted in the execution of the mutineers.

Although British armies won battles, they were no closer to defeating the Continentals, who used guerrilla warfare, slowly eliminating British soldiers, with no replacements for the British soldiers available in North America. The fighting squeezed the local people between the Continental and British forces. Troops from both sides raided farms, absconding with food, clothing, and valuables. Local farmers were unhappy with wartime taxation, loss of livestock and aggression of well-trained British soldiers.

American women often traveled with their husbands in the Continental armies, which helped to reduce the number of Continental deserters. Involvement of the women helped to nurse the sick and wounded, to clean the hospitals, to prepare meals and do laundry. Other women remained at home, closely observing the British troops, often secretly gathering information about British positions, and passing this information on to Continental troops.

Parliament had ordered British troops to protect loyalists, yet British soldiers often robbed both rebels and loyalists. British troops distrusted the locals, not being able to tell the loyalists from the colonial freedom fighters. Ironically, the British would not allow loyalists to execute the rebels as prisoners of war, for fear that rebels would execute captured British soldiers in revenge. Prisoner exchanges took place, British soldiers for rebel soldiers. British leaders allowed the execution of loyalists, instead of negotiating for the exchange of loyalists. Most loyalists eventually relocated to Canada. Loyalists who remained masqueraded as revolutionaries to avoid rough colonial "justice." Continental Colonel Charles Lynch repeatedly hanged loyalists after quick partisan trials, which originated the term to "lynch' a person.

General Washington finally began to win a war of attrition. When wounded or killed, British army Generals requested more British soldiers by letters sent on ships. The new British soldiers had to be located and enlisted within Britain, then transported back across the Atlantic Ocean. This process could take six months or more.

The movement of British troops into the Southern colonies alienated the local Colonials. As a result, the number of Southern loyalists continuing to support the British declined. The British also encouraged small bands of Native Americans, runaway slaves, and common criminals, to stage raids on Colonials to help supply the British forces. These British army tactics alienated former loyalists who did not want to fight side by side with people they considered disreputable. After the British armies moved on from a particular location, colonial militias returned to that location and exacted revenge against any local persons who had cooperated with the British. As outsiders who were losing battles, the British had little chance to convince Southerners to fight on their side.

When Britain's leaders diverted troops away to protect other British assets around the world from attacks by the French, Spanish and Dutch Navies, fewer troops were available to fight against the Continental soldiers. Britain's forces proved completely inadequate to defend British colonies in the Caribbean. Britain also pulled back navy ships to European waters, fearing French attacks upon the British Isles. At the same time, colonial leaders reduced the number of mercenaries fighting for Britain by offering reprieves to captured British fighters if they would agree to serve 3 years in the Continental armies.

The Colonials posed new naval threats to Britain: Private investors in the colonies financed fast-moving warships called "privateers," which captured British merchant ships and their cargoes. Privateers also made assaults against British naval ships and facilities. In response, the British expanded their navy, dramatically increasing the number of sailors more than 500%, reaching a total of 105,000 British sailors in service 5 years later in 1781.

A turning point in the war was at the Battle of Saratoga in 1777, where Britain lost one-sixth of all its troops in America. The British leaders had not anticipated the difficulties created by traveling so far inland to Saratoga, where the British navy was unable to support the fighting, resulting in victory for the Continental Army.

In February of 1778, after learning of the American victory at Saratoga, the French entered into a treaty with the Americans, creating a military alliance and reducing barriers to trade between France and the Americans. The navies of both France and Spain were also engaged in conflict with British forces around the world. Spain's involvement against the British also helped the American cause.

In 1778, George Washington, his army short of men, endorsed plans by leaders from New England to recruit colonial slaves to fight in the war, promising future freedom, and paying their masters for them. Washington recruited so many slaves, that by the end of the war, 10% of Continental troops were black, willing to fight in return for an opportunity to become free. Washington privately wrote that he was worried about recruiting Black people from the South, as Black people formed a much greater percentage of the population in the South. Washington feared a revolt of the slaves. The Southern states were against allowing the slaves in the South to fight, although a few slaves were already fighting in the place of their masters.

In 1779, to prevent a French attack upon the British colony of Jamaica, Britain ordered 4,000 troops to sail away from the mainland of America to Jamaica. The need to protect their Caribbean colony lessened the number of British troops available to fight against the Continental Army.

LESSON 18: *Late recognition of the value of settlement often fails to resolve disputes under the same terms available prior to fighting. It is essential to fully evaluate the situation, the options, and the reasons for a dispute, well prior to the commitment of forces to fighting. The reality of the war shattered Britain's unfounded optimism for a good outcome. Almost always, a late settlement is much more expensive when one side finally recognizes that it is better to settle than keep fighting.*

Two years after the war started, King George and Parliament recognized their mistakes in failing to settle with the American colonies. King George's new minister, Lord North, lobbied Parliament to offer an agreement to the Americans that would permanently exempt the American colonies from taxation forever. There would have been no war if the British made this offer in 1774. By 1778, the Americans had already reached an alliance with France, which encouraged the Americans to continue fighting for independence. The Americans refused this British offer, which would have returned them to colonial status.

LESSON 19: *Luck is a much bigger factor in creating outcomes than most people recognize. No matter how strong your position, it is always better to settle for an amount appropriate to the strength of your position, eliminating uncertainty which could produce unforeseen negative consequences. The extent of risks from fighting can never be fully known in advance.*

Back in 1775, when the Revolutionary War started, British leaders did not foresee how future conflicts with France and Spain would impair Britain's efforts in America. British leaders now regretted not resolving their disputes with the Colonials earlier. If both sides had agreed to a settlement before the fighting started, the resolution between Britain and the American colonies would have made Britain more secure. Neither the French nor the Spanish would have risked attacking Britain. British leaders had learned about their mistaken assumptions the hard way.

It is always difficult for leaders to weigh the power of unforeseen events, especially after having been successful in the past. Leaders often act rationally based upon known information, but unforeseen events later destroy them. Cardinal Mazarin, France's political leader in the 1600s wrote, "One must not ask if a general is skillful, but whether he is lucky." In other words, luck may play a bigger role than skill in determining the outcome of war.

In 1781, the French sailed ships to Chesapeake Bay from the Caribbean, to confront the British. The French were able to muster these ships because Spain agreed to defend French shipping and interests in the Caribbean. The coalition of France and Spain led to the American victory over the British General Cornwallis' army at Yorktown, Virginia, after which, British leaders recognized that they would not be able to defeat the Continental forces.

France, Britain's long-time opponent, supported the Americans, supplying French ships under the command of the Marquis de Lafayette, which were the deciding factor in the colonial victory over the British at Yorktown, effectively making America the winner of the Revolutionary War. After this defeat, the British public accepted that further fighting was futile. Parliament recognized that the war was unwinnable. British voters elected new leaders in Parliament, and negotiations for peace with American diplomats began in Paris.

British General Cornwallis' defeat and his failure to negotiate to protect the loyalists fighting for him, resulted in a surrender agreement protecting British prisoners of war. Unlike the British troops, loyalists obtained no such protections, and were subject to execution. After learning about the surrender agreement, loyalists stopped supporting the British. Why should they support Britain when the British generals were not supporting and protecting them? The surrender agreement with Britain also failed to protect the Native Americans, which had assisted the British armies.

The resulting settlement was surprisingly beneficial for America. The boundaries of the American nation grew as a result. America also received fishing rights off the coast of Newfoundland, Canada. Americans conceded that they would repay debts incurred from purchasing British merchandise before the war. America also failed to obtain the favored trade status which the colonies enjoyed with Britain before the war.

Newly appointed as Prime Minister for Britain, Lord Shelburne offered this generous settlement to the Americans, believing that increasing the size of America would increase American farming, thereby slowing American industrialization, as a way to limit American manufacturing competition with Britain. Shelburne also hoped that British generosity to the Americans might lead to reunification with Britain later.

Understandably, the French were outraged that the Americans had made this settlement with Britain, as this settlement was likely to erode America's relationship with France, which had supported the Americans during the fighting, hoping to obtain privileged trading rights with America. The French claimed that the British settlement agreement bribed America at the expense of France.

The British public was also outraged by the settlement terms. Their outrage was short-lived as the settlement of the war immediately increased British exports to America, helping to improve economic conditions in Britain. Americans were happy to buy high quality British goods, sold at a better cost than the goods from France.

Ironically, France had taken on too much debt as a result of fighting wars and supporting the Americans. The huge amount of French debt was one of the factors which led to the overthrow of the French monarchy in the French Revolution, less than two decades after the start of the American Revolution. In hindsight, the French should never have supported the American cause, as the French monarchy bankrupted itself into economic collapse from helping the Americans achieve freedom.

After the war ended, patriot mobs menaced loyalists who were attempting to return to their homes. Many loyalists and their slaves resettled in Canada and other parts of the British Empire, although about one-third gradually returned to America after the bad feelings quieted down. Post-war, Americans were forced to pay much higher taxes to their own government after the Revolution than the taxes Britain demanded before the Revolution. The 13 States each imposed their own internal taxes as the only way to finance the debts incurred in the war.

The new Continental government lacked the ability to raise money to pay off debts from fighting the war because it had no ability to directly tax the American people. Instead, the Continental government relied on the individual states to pay their share of debts from the war. Most States did not pay, although New Jersey paid a token amount to the Continental government. Continental military officers, promised pensions whenever the war should end, received nothing from the Continental Congress. The thirteen States of America were in disarray.

Following settlement with Britain, Americans imported more products from Britain than Britain imported from America. Credit in America became tight. The rate of wages for Americans fell 25 percent from pre-revolution levels of compensation. The American governments, both federal and state, stopped printing paper money. Gold and Silver coins were hard to come by. At the same time, individual state governments increased the tax rates for everyone. People in the lower classes often had to pay the same tax rates as the rich, which left the American poor on the brink of starvation.

Having extricated themselves from British domination, none of the citizens of any of the thirteen states were willing to be dominated by a new, unfamiliar central government. The post-war American Confederation lacked sufficient power to force the individual States to do anything. The entire nation risked failing without a formal organization to control how the states would operate and interact. If the thirteen states did not work together to create a unified America, there were other European powers which could take advantage of American vulnerabilities, not just France and Spain, but also the Netherlands and Russia.

British leaders had long ridiculed the American hypocrisy regarding freedom and slavery. But the majority of the population in the American colonies were unwilling to give up the benefits of keeping slaves. Even American patriot Patrick Henry never freed his slaves, despite admitting that slavery was repugnant, and stating that slavery was inconsistent with Christian thought and was destructive to liberty. American colonials had protested about the British making slaves of the colonials, while at the same time, the colonials had few qualms about the enslavement of Black people.

Slavery had become a foundation of the economies of the Southern states, which relied upon slave labor to operate their large plantations. The voters of Virginia, the Carolinas and Georgia would never agree to end slavery, as doing so would harm their economies. Moreover, the majority of Americans believed that the colonies had to stick together after the war. Continuing the dispute about slavery at this time would prevent all of the colonies from unifying. To protect and preserve their own ways of living, American colonial leaders chose to retain the practice of slavery.

The new state governments of the United States, joined under the Articles of Confederation, were at risk to fail. Some States attempted to satisfy their own interests at the expense of their neighbors in other States. Demagogue officials promised the common people redistribution of money from the wealthy citizens within that State.

The 13 States also faced greater post-war expenses to maintain their own defenses from attack from other countries. America no longer had the British navy to protect it. The new American government had hoped to raise money from the sale of Native American lands in the West, but a post-war Native American confederacy arose, fighting against settlers in the western frontiers, interfering with the sale of Native American lands. The money generated by these land sales was supposed to fund the operation of the American federal government. There was no additional money to fund armies to protect the settlers in the West. The new American Confederation was weak.

The 13 States risked fighting wars with each other, which if not prevented, could have led to a complete breakdown of the Continental government, creating an easy opportunity for the conquest of individual states by one or more of the European powers. There was concern that conflict between States might result in civil war, where the larger States were likely to dominate smaller States. Not surprisingly, smaller States favored the creation of a strong central federal government to protect them from aggression from larger states. As immigration from European countries increased, there was also concern that new Western settlers would try to form their own states, not as a part of the American Confederation, instead joining with Britain, Spain, or other colonizing nations.

Americans who came from Europe strongly favored taking land from the Native Americans. Conflicts with Britain continued over land sales and the forts which the British had retained as part of the settlement of the war. The British claimed that the Americans were violating the terms of the settlement of the war. Britain sought to preserve a physical presence in America, in the event that the new American government disintegrated. Retaining control over their forts could allow the British an opportunity to reclaim authority over America if the new American Confederation of States failed.

Massachusetts farmers, unable to pay their debts, protested by physically blocking the courts to prevent lawsuits from creditors seeking to foreclose on their farms and sell off livestock. Other protestors unsuccessfully attempted to steal firearms from a federal armory. Massachusetts troops battled with the protestors, jailing sixteen men, and executing two others.

Wealthy Americans responded to these troubling events by advocating for a strong national government with more power to control the individual States. James Madison argued that a popular majority could be just as tyrannical as any monarch. Madison supported a federal government which could interact directly with the people of all States, and which would be supreme over the States, where the interests of the nation were concerned.

If the States could not join together to form a popular government, one concern was that an American monarch might unify the states. A second possibility was that multiple Confederations might arise in different sections of North America, fighting with each other and fighting with European nations about land and resources, in a never-ending series of wars.

The Founding Fathers who created the American Constitution in 1789 were wealthy, educated farmers, merchants and lawyers. They wanted to preserve the pre-war economic system which already existed. They would not agree to populist demands seeking to eliminate debts. The Founding Fathers negotiated and eventually created a unique Constitution which, along with the later-adopted Bill of Rights, sufficiently satisfied all American interests by balancing power between states and the federal government, with the aim to satisfy the common people as well as the wealthy. Voters selected officials to lead within each state.

The American wealthy tended to congregate in big cities and seaports, where most newspapers were located, so they had an advantage in shaping news stories and public opinion, as news editors tended to agree with their advertisers and subscribers. Even though there were more farmers than wealthy Americans, the farmers' locations in rural areas caused them to receive news too late to do anything to influence these political events. The wealthy organized and moved quickly in each of the States for ratification of the Constitution. The States which were holding out against ratification saw that they would be in the minority. They feared what might happen to them if left out of the Union. All thirteen States eventually ratified the Constitution, but conflicts of the American States with each other and with the American federal government continue to this day.

The federalist economic policies authored by Alexander Hamilton stabilized the American monetary system. The federal assumption of the debts of each state allowed tax cuts to take place within each state. These and other financial changes caused a boom in American business. Improvements in trade arose from political stability, although the federalist supporters and the states' rights supporters remained in constant conflict.

If the thirteen colonies had been able to make an agreement with the British to avoid fighting before the Revolution, they would have avoided the problems of protecting and maintaining the new, weak American government. We will never know for sure how things would have turned out if the 13 Colonies and Britain had reached a settlement prior to the Revolutionary War, but it is by no means clear that fighting for American independence was the best choice for the 13 Colonies.

All that leaders can do is make rational decisions based upon the information at hand, hoping for the best. Twists of fate and pure luck are unpredictable. The consensus of most historians is that the British blundered unprepared into a Revolutionary War because the British never imagined that they would have to fight. Fear was driving British efforts to control the American colonies, fear that their economy would suffer if the American colonies became independent. In hindsight, this concern was not valid. Although fighting and losing the war temporarily impaired its economy, Britain became more powerful after the Revolutionary War. Its leaders had learned to focus on problem-solving and rational evaluation of outcomes.

The failure of British leaders to protect Britain's best interests led to a disastrous outcome of the war: 43,000 British lives were lost; the national debt of Britain doubled over the 8 years of war; The war cost Britain 80 million British Pounds, which was 7 times the amount of the pre-revolution entire yearly budget for Britain's government for one year.

The Americans did not do better in the aftermath of the Revolutionary War. America's *per capita* income fell 50% during the Revolutionary War. Even as late as 1804, more than 20 years after the war ended, per capita income in America remained 15% lower than it had been before the Revolutionary War. The long-term good news for America was much better: attaining the freedom to expand America westward eventually made America the richest and most powerful country in the world two centuries later.

In addition to Britain's financial losses, 75,000 colonial loyalists fled from America; Britain lost 2,500,000 of its subjects, who became citizens of the newly formed United States of America. Britain also lost 500,000 square miles of its Empire in North America.

Both Britain and the colonials might have been much better off financially If there had been no interruption in American trade with Britain, which impaired the economies of both sides for 40 years after the fighting began. American colonials might have been able to reach an agreement with Britain for gradual independence, thereby avoiding the Revolutionary War and the War of 1812. Financial growth and population growth in America might have continued unabated during those 40 years after 1783. America may have become a much more powerful country sooner, and a political alliance with Britain could have protected both Britain and America from European aggression going forward.

The United States underwent an economic crisis for the first 15 years after the Revolutionary War and continued to experience challenging times until the end of the War of 1812 with Britain, when America returned to explosive economic and population growth.

One positive that resulted from the war of the American Revolution was the creation of the American representative democracy, in response to the oppressive British rule. The leaders of the new American government were well-read in ancient history. They understood the potential danger posed by the form of government called "pure democracy" first documented in ancient Greece. The word "pure" describes a type of democracy where 51 percent of the voters in an election determine all decisions. Each succeeding election can completely change the way a government works. There is no stability over time in a "pure" democratic system of government.

History has consistently shown that "pure" democracies usually lead to rapid collapse of the government. Imagine if every time there were an election in America, 51 percent of the people could vote to change how the entire system of government worked, and then, in the next election, a different 51 percent of the voters could vote to change the entire system of government back to the way it was before. Choosing "pure" democracy has always resulted in chaos. "Pure" democracies usually fail to meet the needs of their people, eventually replaced by military dictatorships, monarchies, or totalitarian governments, as the people who have lived in pure democracies tend to revolt in response to its inherent chaos. The collapse of democracies is followed by citizens of a nation supporting other forms of governments which promise stability, although usually, when a pure democracy collapses, a powerful fascist or monarchal government initially takes its place, providing stability at the expense of individual freedom, as demonstrated in France, following the collapse of the revolutionary government when Napoleon became Emperor.

Having been aware of the past failures of "pure" democracies, the founders of the American Constitution created the unique form of American "representative" democracy, which provides that voters elect leaders to make decisions for them, with checks and balances of power divided between the executives (presidents, governors), legislatures (senators, congressmen, assemblymen) and judiciary (judges). Splitting up the power of American government into different branches has so far prevented any single faction or bad actor from a single branch of the government from hijacking of the entire American government. Tyranny is not possible with American democracy, so long as America's citizens are willing to support the operations of their democratic system and allow the different branches of the American government to keep each other in check.

The inability of elected officials to make changes quickly preserves stability in American-style democracy. Fundamental changes in the structure of American government require a constitutional amendment, where a large majority of the voters must agree with fundamental changes. Due to the stability of the American government, day-to-day life in America continues with less disruption. Major changes take place slowly, through the passage of laws and through the decisions of courts.

America was again on a path to economic prosperity between the War of 1812 and the onset of the American Civil War in 1861. Conflicts arose over time, especially as America expanded westward, creating challenges for the American people. It is important to understand America's transition up to the time of the Civil War, in order to understand the causes that led to the Civil War.

After the American Constitution was ratified, American founding fathers Thomas Jefferson and James Madison were concerned that the British laws of inheritance, including the doctrine of Primogeniture, already a part of the American legal system, would encourage the development of an American aristocracy, similar to the aristocracy of Britain, where a small number of powerful British families controlled almost all of the land. Primogeniture required that the first-born son must inherit all of the father's property, preserving the size and power of the father's estate. Primogeniture prohibited dividing an estate between heirs. Primogeniture also prohibited the sale of any property belonging to an estate or plantation.

Jefferson and Madison were concerned that limiting the number of owners of estates and plantations would concentrate substantial political power in the few owners, who could unfairly use their wealth and power to dominate the politics of the United States, undermining the new American system of government.

Accordingly, in 1796, the laws of the 13 States eliminated Primogeniture, allowing estates, including all property of estates, to be divided and sold. This change had the desired effect of spreading out American wealth and political power among a much greater number of people. Unfortunately, as often happens with changes, unforeseen consequences arose.

Although ending Primogeniture loosened restrictions on buying and selling property, Southern Planters were now free to sell slave property—men, women, and children-- for profit. Many Planters did not maintain family units of their slaves. These Planters soon sold individual slaves, including women of child-bearing age, to owners of new plantations in Western territories. After Primogeniture ended, more Virginians owned slaves and supported expanding slavery. In pursuit of profits, slave owners ignored the inhumanity of splitting up families, whose members would never again have contact with each other.

A cultural divide had long existed between North and South: Southerners embraced the tradition of Chivalry, where noble landlords controlled their serfs, just as the Planters controlled their slaves. The Planters saw themselves as inheritors of European nobility, proud to be descendants of the Norman conquerors who had wrested control of England from the inferior Anglo-Saxon inhabitants of England in the year 1066. Southerners boldly proclaimed their superiority over Northerners, convinced that they would easily defeat armies from the North in any military conflict, if forced to fight to preserve their way of life.

Despite its obvious brutality, the majority of Americans accepted slavery at that time, based upon unfounded beliefs that some races were superior, and other races were inferior and could be subjected to slavery.

At the beginning of colonization, indentured servants performed most labor for colonial landowners. In return for transport to America, these servants would work for a set number of years as indentured servants, then receive cash or land to continue their lives independent of their employers. Over time, the African slave trade developed as the economies of Britain and America grew, driven by the demand for sugar grown in the Caribbean islands. Demand for African slave labor rose, as it became apparent to the Planters that it was more profitable to use African slaves as opposed to using indentured servants. The African slaves would work their entire lives and did not require the owners to make a payment after a limited number of years of service. Moreover, the Planters convinced themselves that Black slaves were sub-human and, therefore, did not require humane treatment. The Planters' focus was to generate profits. Cruelty and inhumane treatment of slaves was common.

Motivated to colonize the Southern States to become wealthy, Leaders in the South prospered by developing large plantations, modeled after the earlier Caribbean plantations, growing tobacco and cotton, as the mainland climate of Virginia, the Carolinas and Georgia was not warm enough to produce sugar. European demand for tobacco and cotton rapidly grew, providing the Southern Planters with great wealth and lifestyles modeled after European feudal lords. Each Planter had his own estate. He maintained large numbers of slave workers with minimal interference from government. The Planters attained the political power which comes with wealth, and working together, they successfully controlled the politics of the particular States in which they lived.

In the early 1800s, Planters sold slaves far away from their families, often taken to the western territories of America, to clear the wilderness land and create more plantations. Wealthy Planters increased their wealth by acquiring more land and growing more cotton and tobacco.

In 1807, Britain banned the African slave trade, as the British public was rightly outraged at the terrible conditions slaves suffered during transport to the colonies, resulting in a high number of fatalities. In 1808, The United States also banned importing slaves, but allowed the practice of slavery to continue within the American nation.

Demand for slave labor increased after America outlawed slave importation. Due to the inability of Planters to purchase additional slaves from Africa, the prices for slaves currently living in the South and West of America rose as high as 50%. Plantation owners sold their slaves to distant purchasers who would pay the highest price, regardless of the pain created by the slaves' separation from their families and friends.

During this time, Congress passed immigration laws encouraging white people from Europe to settle in America. These same laws prohibited Black people from settling in America. At the same time, a growing number of people in Europe and America wanted to completely abolish slavery for religious reasons. The New England States had the greatest number of these Abolitionists who actively spoke out against the inhumanity of slavery. This is not surprising as the people who came to America in pursuit of religious freedom founded the New England States. Unlike the Planters, these Northerners had few slaves, and believed it was their religious obligation to perform labor themselves to create their communities, prospering through hard work and thrift.

The New Englanders had little use for slaves on their smaller farms, where they intended to perform the work themselves. In contrast, the Southern colonies were purely profit-making ventures, copying the manner of operation of the Caribbean sugar colonies, where small numbers of Europeans had transported vast numbers of slaves to the islands, many dying, crammed into ships with inadequate food, ventilation, and sanitation while in transport. More slaves died due to tropical diseases and over-work in the hot Caribbean climate, with little care or concern received from their European owners.

Trained in the Caribbean plantations, the Planters who migrated to the newer colonies in the Carolinas had ambitions to become rich, motivated by the opportunities located in the much larger, unsettled lands of the American continent.

The conflict between the ideologies of the Southern Planters and the Northern Abolitionists increased over time, as the number of slaves in America doubled. Southern political leaders wanted to extend the practice of slavery to the western territories and to any new States entering the Union.

As the number of States in America increased, additional disputes arose between the Northern and Southern States, each side attempting to gain, or at least maintain, their own political power. The Three/Fifths compromise was made a part of the American Constitution, giving the Southern States increased political power by being able to count three-fifths of each slave as a "person" in determining the number of people in each State for purposes of representation in Congress.

Due to the onset of the Industrial Revolution, immigration from Europe to the industrial Northern states surpassed immigration to the Southern states. When Southerners moved west and developed new plantations in Missouri, they applied for Missouri statehood as a slave state, which triggered strong opposition from the Northern states, whose citizens objected to the extension of slavery. When the territory of Maine also applied to become a separate state that would not allow slavery, the Missouri Compromise of 1820 admitted both Missouri and Maine to the Union, preserving the balance of power regarding the slavery issue within the United States.

Other disputes arose between the Northern States and the Southern States, creating a political movement in the South seeking the formation of a separate Southern nation. These disputes arose as the size and nature of America dramatically changed in the 80 years after the American Revolution. America had grown much larger. Modern technology had changed the way people lived.

PART 3: The American Civil War— Refusal to Change

"It should have been different
It could have been easy
But too much money rolled in to ever end slavery
The cry for war spread like wildfire"

– Lyrics from the
Watchhouse song, "Wildfire"
Written by Andrew Marlin

The balance of power within the United States tipped in favor of the Northern States over the Southern States due to increases in the Northern population. The weather in the North was not conducive to growing cotton. The valuable waterpower of the Northern States encouraged the expansion of manufacturing, using the technology of the Industrial Revolution. The need for factory workers in the Northern States attracted large groups of Europeans to migrate to the Northern States for a better life than in Europe.

Poor economies and bleak prospects in Europe motivated people to emigrate to America, the most arrived from Ireland and Germany. They made their way to the rapidly developing Northern Midwest, attracted to work in new factories, powered by the plentiful, fast-flowing rivers driven by the high elevations of the North. On average, Southern lands in coastal areas were more level than in the North.

Their slower rivers provided less waterpower. Understandably, the number of factories built in the South was less, as there was less waterpower to drive the new factory machinery that inventors were creating. There were fewer jobs for immigrants in the South, due to extensive slave labor. The Planters were not interested in paying European immigrants wages for their labor.

The opening of the Erie Canal in New York State in 1825 allowed shipping barges to transport goods and people in the North much more quickly between the Great Lakes and New York City. The Erie Canal dramatically reduced the cost of transport, compared to the expense of hauling goods and people along muddy roads, using wagons with teams of horses. On the Erie Canal, there was less risk of attack from criminals or Native Americans along the way. Over time, railroad networks also developed throughout the North, leading to the West, enabling immigrants to settle in the Midwest quickly and safely, at less expense.

Southern leaders understood that the increases in the populations of the Northern States threatened the political power of the Southern States. It was inescapable that these new European migrants would vote, giving the Northern States the power to dominate national elections in the future.

The Planters understandably feared that the loss of political power would eventually result in slavery ending throughout the United States, threatening their prosperity and the Southern way of life. Northern voters might also attempt to expand Federal power, interfering with the States' rights, which the South had fought to retain, during the drafting of the United States Constitution.

Population remained the main source of every nation's power. Adding immigrants to its population increased a nation's power to muster men to fight in wars. Success in fighting wars depended on the number of soldiers any nation could bring to the fight. Battles were competitions of attrition: The side with the most soldiers eventually won. Soldiers from opposing sides died or could no longer fight, due to disease, starvation or wounds sustained in battle. At that time, the lack of scientific understanding in the field of medicine allowed twice the number of soldiers to die from disease or physical hardship in war, compared to the number of soldiers killed as a direct consequence of battle.

Keep in mind that the United States Constitution created a Union with limited Federal power, with more powers remaining vested in the individual States. One of the goals of the Founding Fathers of the United States was to limit Federal governmental power by dividing it between the three branches of the new American federal government. The Founding Fathers understood that unrestrained Federal governmental power threatened the freedom of the common people of each State. The new American Constitution retained the majority of the political power within the individual States. The power of the Federal government and the President was limited by States' rights.

LESSON 21: *People who make arrogant claims of racial and cultural superiority have a propensity to start wars, believing that their superior abilities will guarantee victory.*

Slavery supported the profitable Southern plantations which grew and exported cotton to England and France. The Industrial Revolution created new inventions, increasing the output of goods. International markets for manufactured cotton cloth grew due to strong demand. England and France developed extensive textile manufacturing, selling enormous quantities of finished cloth world-wide. To satisfy the tremendous demand for manufactured cloth, England and France dramatically increased their purchases of American cotton, the sale of which created great wealth for the Planters. Seeking to increase profits, the Planters sought to own more slaves, to be able to produce and sell even greater quantities of cotton.

By the time the Civil War started in 1861, the economy of the Southern States had grown to become the fourth largest economy in the world. It is not surprising that Southern leaders aggressively defended their new-found wealth. The Planters had a "gold-rush" enthusiasm to produce more cotton, which clouded their thinking and blinded them to the horrors of slavery. The Planters egotistically attributed their prosperity to superior intelligence and business practices, rather than timing and luck which, in reality, had produced their wealth. The invention of the cotton gin, combined with the rapid growth of markets for cotton cloth, made the Southern Planters rich and powerful.

Southern leaders disparaged the wage-labor system of the Northern states, proclaiming that working for wages was worse than slavery. Visitors from Europe could not help but notice that the cities and buildings of the North were in superior condition compared to those in the South. The mansions of the Planters were magnificent, but other southern buildings and roads were in disrepair. Slaves in the South lived in decrepit housing and survived on minimal sustenance. The Planters did not see any value created by spending their profits to improve the living conditions of their slaves. There was no pathway for slaves to better themselves or escape their desperate existence. They were at the mercy of their masters. Planters often treated their slaves as though they were animals.

Before the Civil War, deep divides developed throughout America relating to slavery. Although it is hard for us to believe now, the reality then was that a majority of voters in both the Northern States and the Southern States were in favor of allowing slavery to continue where it already existed in America.

As the national elections of 1860 approached, Southern leaders threatened to secede from the Union of the United States to form their own separate Confederation. Other people in the North, in the Border states and also in the South, insisted on maintaining the Union intact. A division of the Union into separate parts would risk war and conflict, not only between the separated parts of the Union, but also risked invasion from other nations. Splitting the Union would weaken all of its former parts, inhibiting settlement of the territories in the West. European colonizing nations might invade the Pacific coastal lands if the United States failed to expand in that direction.

Southern leaders were confident that they could succeed in creating and maintaining a Confederate nation. Why shouldn't the founding of a Southern Confederation be successful? The American Constitution was silent on the issue of whether States could voluntarily withdraw from the Union.

Pro-Union advocates believed that Southern secession would harm America's international standing. Leaders of nations around the world would believe that the people of the United States were not capable of maintaining a republican democracy. A division of the American nation would prove the failure of American democracy, with the remnants of the United States weakened and in disarray.

Despite the North having a population twice as large as the population of the South, it was not at all certain that the Union would win a Civil War and successfully prevent the secession of the Southern states from forming a separate nation.

The North had a much greater capacity to manufacture goods, including weapons, uniforms, and accessories for their soldiers. The Northern states had built far more railroads than existed in the South, which gave the North much greater capacity to manufacture parts to resupply and rebuild railroads if and when they were damaged or destroyed in the fighting. They also had a larger number of horses and mules for the transport of soldiers and supplies.

The Union had its own limitations: At the start of the War, the Union maintained a small army and a small navy, both spread out across the immense American lands and coastlines. The design of the ships of the Union Navy enhanced travel along coastal areas, yet the Civil War naval battles would take place in rivers, which required ships with more maneuverability, designed to operate in shallow waters.

Given the fixed attitudes of the Planters, there is no way they ever would have agreed to negotiate to try to obtain concessions without fighting. Negotiation before fighting could not be successful. Yet, the Civil War is instructive regarding the difficulties for both sides created by reliance on assumptions each had prior to the fighting. Even if early mediation of the conflicts would have been fruitless, airing of the problems might have allowed both sides to have acted differently as the conflict intensified.

When the American Civil War started, States located on the border line between the Northern and Southern States, known as the Mason-Dixon line, tended to have blended interests. At the beginning of the war, these Border States were Delaware, Kentucky, Maryland, and Missouri. Depending on the particular issue at hand, each of these States might agree with the Union or with the Confederate positions. The Border States remained neutral during the Civil War. Depending on how the war proceeded, if one or more of the Border States decided to change their political stance, this action could have made the difference between victory and defeat for either the Union or for the Confederacy. As with most "real-world" disputes, the issues were complicated, not clear-cut, "us or them," or "good guys vs. bad guys."

The practice of slavery was a horror, a stain on the conscience of the United States. But at the time the Civil War started, the majority of American citizens in both the North and South had prejudices regarding the non-white races. At that time, America had four million Black slaves out of a total United States population of thirty-two million people. The United States was the largest slave-holding country in the world. There were free Black people in the North, but the vast majority of Black people in the United States were slaves.

When slavery began in the United States, there were more Native Americans made slaves by the colonizing Europeans than any other race. It was only over time, primarily through the efforts of the Planters, that Africans' skin color came to identify them as slaves in America. The Planters benefitted from this "color" identification as more Black slaves were brought to America. It was easier for Plantation owners to maintain order and identify runaway slaves if all of their slaves were Black.

British and French colonizers in the Caribbean islands had used slave labor to grow sugar long before new plantations developed in the North American mainland. Farmers in the cooler climates of the North could not grow the most profitable crops of the Southern States, such as tobacco, rice, and indigo. The South's warm climate was perfect for growing these crops using slave labor on a large scale.

Southern leaders rationalized the cruelty of slavery, claiming that Black people were less than human, that Black people were made for the use of whites, that Black people wanted to be controlled by whites, and that Black people loved slavery in the same way that Whites loved freedom. It was ridiculous, but Southern Planters made those pronouncements at that time, to support their interests in maintaining slavery.

The Planters expressed outrage that Abolitionists in the Northern states aggressively sought to outlaw slavery everywhere in America. New England's religious leaders preached egalitarianism, supported by European immigrants seeking religious freedom. Abolitionists preached against slavery, against Plantation owners breaking up slave families and selling young slaves to plantations far away from their relatives. They spoke out against whipping and other barbaric punishments used by Southern planters.

Once the United States had prohibited further importation of slaves into the United States in 1808, the only way to fill their demand for more slaves was for Planters to encourage their slaves to have more children. The Planters profited by breeding their slaves as though they were horses and cattle, then selling slave children and young adults to other plantations. The accelerating demand for cotton cloth around the world caused the value of slaves to rise dramatically in America. They had become highly valuable property.

In the years approaching the start of the American Civil War, the population of settlers increased in the western territories, which America soon added as new States. A national political controversy raged. Abolitionists wanted to outlaw slavery in the new States. Southern leaders believed that it was important for any new State to be able to choose on its own whether or not to allow the practice of slavery.

In 1850, eleven years before the start of the Civil War, Congress passed the federal Fugitive Slave Act, supported by political pressure from leaders of the Southern states, allowing Planters to retrieve slaves who had escaped, and traveled North to become free. This Fugitive Slave Act created bounties and money payments, incentives to return fugitive slaves to their masters. The Fugitive Slave Act also imposed harsh penalties upon anyone assisting slaves to escape from their masters.

The effect of the Fugitive Slave Act was to allow Southerners to travel to Northern States and undertake kidnappings and forcible enslavement of Black people, many of whom had not been slaves and were lawfully free. Both runaway slaves and free Black people were arrested, and taken South anyway, where all were enslaved. Passage of this law and its validation by the Supreme Court at that time, had the effect of motivating more American voters to favor the total abolition of slavery.

There were no restrictions in most States regarding the sale of slaves. Not all Planters were willing to break up slave families, but the practice of breaking up slave families was common enough to become scandalous. With the publication of Harriet Beecher Stowe's anti-slavery novel <u>Uncle Tom's Cabin</u> in 1851, more voters in the North supported outlawing all slavery. At the same time, the Southern leaders made it illegal to possess or sell a copy of <u>Uncle Tom's Cabin</u> in the South, as the novel depicted Southern Planters as being cruel and inhumane.

LESSON 22: *A book can change the world.*

HARRIET BEECHER
STOWE
(Photo from The
Smithsonian)

Harriet Beecher Stowe's writing helped to end slavery in the United States. She had been born into a wealthy family at a time when women were possessions of their husbands, with no right to vote. She labored to become a skillful writer and teacher, embracing the opportunities which came her way.

She was the youngest of seven children born to a well-known preacher. When she was growing up in the 1830s, women had almost no chance to have careers or be independent. Harriet was lucky that her older sister Catherine had founded a female Seminary in Hartford, Connecticut, when Harriet was 13 years old.

The purpose of the female seminary was to educate young women to the same degree as young men, to be able to think for themselves and to have greater influence on their own lives. There, as a young student, Harriet learned to teach, preach, and write, in a place where women mutually instructed each other. She became the Editor of the school newspapers. When she graduated from her sister's seminary, Harriet stayed on as a teacher of composition and rhetoric, subjects we now call writing and speech. Her teaching job allowed Harriet to further her own reading and studies. She wanted to "morally influence" others. By age 18, Harriet had become a confident public speaker. She also counseled other young women.

The Beecher family moved from Hartford to the fast-growing midwestern city of Cincinnati, Ohio in 1832. At that time, Cincinnati was a center of trade, located at the Ohio River. There Harriet wrote children's books and also published articles in magazines. She made substantial money from her writing, while teaching school at the same time. Harriet married and had six children over the next 18 years. She continued to study and write, running her household with assistance from Black servants.

In Cincinnati, Harriet joined a literary club, where the members all wrote and read their work aloud to the others, as a form of entertainment. (There was no radio or television for entertainment at this time.) The members of the literary club provided valuable feedback regarding Harriet's writing. She paid attention to their suggestions, and her writing style improved, as did her ability to influence her readers.

Harriet's husband was an Abolitionist college professor who was vocal about ending slavery at a time when mobs were rioting and harming Abolitionists. Harriet wanted to protect free speech. She despised mob violence and how it could spread to upset the established order. She wrote anti-slavery articles for newspapers under a masculine pen name. Harriet did not publish under her own name as she remained conservative regarding the role of women in America.

As the years progressed, Harriet authored fictional stories involving social issues, such as drunkenness, using Christian themes of moral and cultural reform, featured in a popular women's magazine. By 1842, she was able to publish a book of her previously written short stories under her own name. It was unusual for women to be authors at that time. Harriet's popularity was due to her ability to produce content that her audience wanted to read, with a writing style that pleased most people.

Harriet understood the need to attack corrupt systems, but wisely, she did not attack specific people. She believed the problem was not people but, rather, embracing the wrong principles. Harriet's frequent discussions with her Black servants about their family problems gave her the plot material for writing Uncle Tom's Cabin. One of Harriet's servants had escaped from the south. Her master had come looking for her. Harriett's husband and her father helped this servant escape to Canada by using the "Underground Railroad," a term that described a system of hidden transport of runaway slaves from home to home of Abolitionists. Runaways used the "Underground Railroad" to travel to Canada, where they could live free, as slavery was neither allowed nor recognized in Canada.

Harriet created a fictional novel to publicize the horrors of the Fugitive Slave Act, even though she had only written short works of fiction before. This novel, Uncle Tom's Cabin, was first distributed in serial chapters appearing on a weekly basis in a national magazine over a period of nine months. Uncle Tom's Cabin described how Black people felt and lived at that time, through the perspective of a white woman. Harriet created characters that came alive on the written pages, using plotting based upon the stories she had heard and accounts of real incidents which had appeared in the newspapers of that time. Harriet's fictional <u>Uncle Tom's Cabin</u> had an emotional punch. The effect of this book was to encourage more Americans to take a stand against slavery.

The publisher collected all of the serialized chapters of <u>Uncle Tom's Cabin</u> in a book with that title, selling 10,000 copies in the first week and 300,000 copies in the first year of publication. No author in either Europe or America had ever earned so much money from the sale of a book. <u>Uncle Tom's Cabin</u> became an international best-selling book, unifying and expanding the Abolitionist movement in America and around the world.

Years later, during the American Civil War, upon meeting Harriet Beecher Stowe, Abraham Lincoln said to her: "So you are the little lady that started this war!" No one had done more to bring the issue of slavery to a head than Harriet Beecher Stowe. She became a celebrity and went on to lead a full and long life, writing and traveling around the world.

Despite this growing Abolitionist movement, Southern leaders pursued extending slavery to new Western states and territories, unconcerned that their path might lead to military conflict with the North. The majority of Southern leaders saw no need to negotiate with the Northern leaders.

While the Southern states' economies had continued to boom unabated, the North had suffered a major financial downturn in 1857, three years before the Civil War began. Southern leaders believed that their own slave labor system was immune from the type of economic downturn which had harmed the economy of the Northern States. Confident that their financial system was efficient and profitable, Southern leaders would not tolerate any additional limitations upon slavery. They would never yield to the "Tyranny of the North," believing that the powers reserved to the States in the Constitution gave the Southern States the right to be independent, should they choose to secede.

Knowing that Europe's textile-driven economies were dependent on the South supplying copious quantities of highly valuable cotton, Southern leaders anticipated that they could rely upon Britain and France for financial and military support, helping to create an independent Southern Confederacy. France had assisted the rebels in the successful American Revolution, so Southern leaders believed that they could expect the same degree of support from France to preserve the Southern way of life.

The class system present in the South was similar to the systems of classes of Britain and France. Southern leaders believed that the expansion of slavery into new states was a good thing and that slave labor was a better system than the wage system. They claimed that Northern laborers led a lower-class, wage-slave way of life. This way of thinking is incomprehensible to us today. Closing their minds to the idea that slavery would eventually end in the civilized world, the Planters stubbornly defended their way of life.

No open-minded person with a conscience could accept the inhumanity of slavery. Southern leaders ignored the ever-increasing pressure to end slavery around the world, primarily because the Southern leaders' affluent lifestyle and the ability of their descendants to be successful depended upon the continuation of slavery.

The Missouri Compromise of 1820 had limited the extension of slavery into new States. Then in 1854, passage of the Kansas-Nebraska Act repealed the Missouri Compromise. This extended slavery on a State-by-State basis in those States which voted to allow it. The possibility of new States expanding the practice of slavery outraged Northern voters, setting the stage for the Civil War to begin 7 years later.

Before the Civil War began, total abolition of slavery was so unpopular that New York Senator William Seward, a front-running candidate for President who had acknowledged that he believed in Abolition, was not chosen as the candidate for President of the newly formed Republican Party, because Seward could not achieve a majority and be elected. The majority of voters in the North did not support Abolition. Seward also supported the rights of Catholics. His pro-Catholic stance hurt his electability as the majority of Americans saw the Pope as an enemy of American governmental power at the time.

A newcomer to national politics, Abraham Lincoln became the republican candidate for president in 1860, and won the presidential election. Lincoln had promised to fight against any extension of slavery into the new States in the West. He became President in 1860 promising to hold the United States together, to preserve the Union, to keep the entire country intact and strong, securing the United States from risk of invasion by European nations.

At the same time, Lincoln promised to allow slavery to continue in the South as it had existed before, until an agreement could be reached for a solution to gradually eliminate slavery. Lincoln would not have been chosen as the republican candidate if he supported Abolition. The Republican leaders chose Lincoln as their candidate because he did not seek to outlaw slavery. Lincoln's priority was keeping the United States intact, essential for the future security and prosperity of the North and South.

The practice of slavery had been retained in order to join the thirteen States together after the Revolutionary War. Otherwise, the Founding Fathers could not have created a Union of States. Lincoln knew that continuing slavery embarrassed the United States. The newspapers in Europe voiced the hypocrisy of allowing slavery to exist in the "land of the free." Lincoln believed that slavery would eventually end in every nation in the world.

The promise of America was that someone could start at the bottom of the economic ladder, just as Lincoln had done, yet work hard for himself to live well and save money, and to better himself as a person. Lincoln defined the concept of "liberty" as the freedom of a man to do what he wanted with himself and with the products of his own labor. Lincoln believed that people who worked should be able to keep the fruits of their own labor. Slavery gave the fruits of slaves' labor to their masters. Slaves could never better their own lives. Lincoln had traveled to New Orleans, Louisiana as a young man and was upset at the cruelty of slave auctions he had observed.

In 1854, seven years before the start of the Civil War, Lincoln gave a speech in which he declared that he hated the monstrous industry of slavery. He abhorred the hypocritical Planter concept of "freedom" which gave men the power to interfere with the freedom of other men, as well as the power to seize the benefits of the labor of other men.

Yet, Lincoln understood the resistance of the Southern leaders, as their economic well-being depended upon slave labor. Lincoln stated that, eventually, the United States would be all slave or all free. There could be no middle ground.

Before he became President, Lincoln authored a plan for the Union government to fund a gradual buyout of slaves from slave owners. Buyouts were not new: In 1833, less than 30 years before the start of the American Civil War, Britain had outlawed slavery within Britain and had paid huge sums of money to slave owners as compensation for the loss of their slave property. Lincoln much preferred for the United States to incur the expense of a slave buyout, compared to the much greater expense of fighting a war over slavery, not to mention the loss of life, which was inevitable in war. In both the Northern States and the Southern States, however, political support for a slave buyout was lacking. Lincoln's plan for a slavery buyout was a non-starter.

A majority of voters in the North and in the South were strongly against the idea of the American government paying the Planters to free their slaves. Voters in the North were afraid of what might happen when slavery ended. What would happen to Northern cities if millions of freed slaves arrived all at once? How would the massive migration of slaves from the South affect the economy and change the way of life in the North?

Poor Irish and German immigrants who had settled in the Northern States feared that a huge migration of former Black slaves would compete for work in factories, driving down wages and reducing the opportunities for Irish and German immigrants to find work and to thrive in America. It is important to remember that there were no government safety nets at that time. Obtaining work was the only way to earn money to pay for food and shelter. Charity was private, dispensed mostly by churches and other religious organizations.

Most people of the North lacked familiarity with Black people, as there were far fewer Black people in the North. These Northerners believed the propaganda generated by Southern leaders that Black people were inferior to white people and would disrupt life in the North.

LESSON 23: *Large disputes are usually many-sided, with multiple factions existing on each side. Any faction has the potential to derail a settlement for their side. The representatives of each side usually have to check back with their own people before committing to any change in position. The leaders of each side need to achieve a solution to satisfy as many of their factions as possible.*

The wealthy Planters easily dominated the politics in the Southern States and faced little opposition. Once Abraham Lincoln became President of the United States, the legislatures of several Southern states voted to secede from the United States. These leaders rapidly drafted their own separate Constitution, creating the Confederate States of America, declaring themselves to be leaders of a new nation. They anticipated that more States would soon join the Confederacy, and prosper, free of any interference from the Union.

Before the Civil War began, most Americans agreed with the need to keep the Union together. But to the leaders in the South, retaining their way of life was more important than concern about attacks from world powers. The Planters' greatest motivations were to guarantee that they would continue to enjoy the way of life they already possessed, and to prevent domination by voters in the North.

Despite the South having only one-half of the population size of the North, the Confederates were confident of military success if and when the South ceased to be a part of the Union. The South had trained soldiers equal in number to the soldiers who were fighting for the North. Southern soldiers had trained at private military schools, such as the Virginia Military Institute, the Citadel as well as at the United States Military Academy at West Point.

Southern leaders underestimated the quality of the troops of the Union, particularly soldiers who had emigrated from Europe. Southern leaders convinced themselves that these Northern soldiers were poor fighters and that one soldier from the South equaled the fighting ability of ten soldiers from the North. The Southerners believed that any military conflict with the North would be over quickly in favor of the South. All of these Southern assumptions proved to be wrong. The rigid mindset of the Southern leaders prevented them from recognizing the risks and uncertainty of a war, prevented them from accepting the idea that they could obtain a better outcome by negotiating with the North.

Southern leaders saw secession from the Union as a natural right of each State as defined in the United States Constitution. They claimed a legitimate right to exercise self-determination, the same right exercised almost one hundred years earlier, when the American colonies rebelled against Britain in the American Revolution. As all the States of the Union had retained powers guaranteed under the federal Constitution, Southern leaders claimed that the Constitution had reserved to all States sufficient power to withdraw from the Union without consequences. The Constitution itself contained no language directly addressing the power of any State to withdraw.

When they finally formed their Confederacy, the leaders of the Southern States recognized the need to build Confederate armies and navy from scratch. Morale of the new armies of Confederate troops was high, as they were fighting to preserve their way of life, protecting their own lands, supported by non-combatant slaves and civilians who provided their soldiers with supplies and reports about the activities of the Northern troops.

Union troops were less motivated to attack Confederate armies, hesitant to enter unfamiliar Southern lands to fight against former allies, many of whom had been friends. The Confederacy encompassed large areas of land, making it more difficult for Union armies to invade. For example, the coastline of the Confederacy ran for 3,500 miles, interrupted by hundreds of rivers, which provided so many hiding places that the Union navy was unable to completely blockade and prevent goods from reaching the Confederates.

The geography of the Appalachian Mountain range also favored the Southern troops, which could easily retreat to the interior of the continent, far away from the east coast of America, unlike Northern troops who had to travel away from coastal areas to chase retreating Southern troops. Roads leading into the Southern interior were few. All roads in the South could be muddy, which interfered with the Union forces' transport of weapons and supplies into Confederate lands.

The North had more than twice the number of potential soldiers compared to the South. But only half of eligible Northern males would eventually serve in the Civil War. The South mobilized a much greater percentage: four out of five men of the South would serve in the Confederate armies.

Ironically, their slaves enabled the Southern soldiers to fight more effectively. Slave servants traveled with the Southern armies, providing support for the troops, performing every type of work and service, with the exception of fighting. Northern soldiers performed the same non-combat work for Union troops that the slaves performed for Southern troops. Other slaves remained at home to help Southern women operate farms, plantations and businesses, assistance that the wives of the Union soldiers did not have.

The North boasted about five times the number of factories than in the South, as well as possessing the advantage of large numbers of factory workers. The most common method of transportation for people and goods at that time was by horse and mule, the North having twice the number available in the South. There were more railroads, ships, and goods produced in the North. The armament factories in the North had superior capacity to manufacture weapons.

The Confederacy had one significant advantage over the Union: It was much easier for the South to defend their own lands than for the Northern armies to attack them. Soldiers of an invading army require ongoing support with weaponry, food, and shelter as long as the fighting continues. When attacked, Southern soldiers committed all their energy and resources to defend their homeland, with support from local civilians. Morale was high as Southern soldiers banded together to fight the common enemy. Local troops were familiar with the geography, and usually had the support of the civilians, who provided additional supplies and relayed information about the actions of the Northern invaders.

When the battles of the Civil War began, the Union armies had difficulties deploying into the Confederate states. Most Confederate roads were dirt, quickly turning to mud as troops and wagons trampled over them. Union troops crept along slowly to reach their military objectives, allowing Union supply wagons sufficient time to follow them into Confederate lands. The large scale of Southern geography helped the Confederate armies to escape from battles with Union armies, particularly at the beginning of the war. Union troops lacked enthusiasm for conflict, which is not surprising, given that the soldiers were fighting against people very much like themselves, who had previously been allies.

Southern fighters did not have to conquer the Union armies to achieve secession. The Confederacy only needed to survive until Union voters became disenchanted with the fighting. Once the Union voters grew tired of losing their young men, they might choose to co-exist with a separate Confederate nation, rather than continuing to fight. Northern troops could not win victory unless they fully defeated the Confederates armies and forced reunion of all the States.

The greatest advantage of the South was its enormous size. The Union would send armed troops and naval vessels to hundreds of destinations, making it difficult to keep their soldiers coordinated and supplied. As Union troops moved inland towards the mountains, away from seacoasts and major rivers, they became vulnerable to surprise attacks and the failure of their supply chains.

The Union Navy attempted to blockade the Confederacy from receiving supplies and goods, but the large, extensive coastlines, rivers and bays of the Atlantic coast left the Union Navy unable to prevent smuggling of arms and supplies into Confederate lands.

President Lincoln made an offer at the beginning of the war, which, if accepted, would have shortened the war, and have avoided carnage. Lincoln sent messengers to General Robert E. Lee shortly after it became clear that war with the South was unavoidable. Lincoln's representatives met with Lee to persuade him to accept the position as chief general for the Union of the United States. One of the most able generals in the United States, also a citizen of Virginia, if Lee could be convinced to fight for the Union, this might convince the State of Virginia to return to the Union and end the Confederacy before it got going. Honor-bound to fight for his native State of Virginia, Lee refused.

General Lee led his Confederate troops to victories over larger Northern armies in the first year of the war. If General Lee had agreed to fight for the Union instead of fighting for the South, the Civil War might have ended in less than one year, instead of lasting four brutal and bloody years. If a mediator could have educated General Lee of the potential for a bad Confederate outcome, the nation might have avoided the Civil War. Lee had the best of intentions. Like most leaders of the South, he did not acknowledge the potential for defeat. Lee believed that chivalry and honor required him to support his home state. He looked no further than to his duty, proceeding to lead Virginia and the rest of the Confederate states down a tragic path with terrible consequences for the South, which none of the Southern leaders could foresee prior to the start of fighting.

It is important to note that mediators view disputes from the perspective of each side to a conflict, in order to resolve the conflict. From the Southern perspective, the loss of the Civil War deprived the South of everything it had hoped to attain by seceding. The Civil War ended in a total disaster for the Planters, which had been avoidable. There is no doubt, however, that the war led to the end of slavery, albeit with tremendous human losses to both sides. The war brought a tremendous victory in the Northern fight against slavery.

In the beginning of the fighting, troops on both sides embraced the prospect of battle with excessive zeal and optimism, looking forward to a new, military way of life. Over time, the appeal of fighting wore off. Boredom, disgusting food, and terrible violence affected soldiers from both sides, who longed to return to their comfortable pre-war lives.

The Confederate victories in the beginning years of the war increased the chances that the Confederacy might well survive the war. During the first 18 months of the war, the Confederate armies won more battles than the Union armies won. Even when a Union army won a battle, the commanding Union general often failed to pursue the defeated Confederate army, which later regrouped and resupplied, and went on to fight in other battles.

In the first two years of fighting, European powers could have recognized the Confederacy as a legitimate nation. If Confederate armies kept winning battles, France and Britain might have interceded in the conflict to support the Confederacy by sending financial aid and troops to force an end to the fighting, and to assist the new Confederate nation.

But the assumptions and arrogance of the leaders of the South created unforeseen problems: As soon as the war began, the Confederate leaders decided to stop exporting cotton, knowing that their main customers in Britain and France depended on American cotton for their extensive clothmaking industries. The Confederate leaders had assumed the need for quantities of cotton to manufacture cloth would motivate France and Britain to break up any Union blockade of Confederate ports.

The South's decision to stop exporting cotton to Europe turned out to have been a major mistake: Instead of helping the Confederate cause, the refusal to trade cotton with Britain and France reduced the taxes collected by the Confederate States from the sale of cotton. The failure to obtain this tax money deprived the Confederacy of substantial funds at a crucial time when the Confederacy faced the expense of building and maintaining armies and navies. Moreover, the South's refusal to provide cotton to Britain and France alienated the leaders of those nations. They were not happy with the Confederate attempt to force Britain and France into conflict with the Union, which was becoming stronger every day, due to population increase.

Due to pre-war years of excess cotton production and importation, France and Britain had already purchased and possessed large supplies of cotton by the time the Civil War began. Britain's leaders adapted to the loss of American cotton by quickly developing its own cotton plantations in Britain's Indian and Egyptian colonies, both of which had climates conducive to growing cotton. These new British plantations in Africa and Asia soon provided sufficient supplies of new cotton to Britain, as stockpiles of Planter cotton ran out. Manufacturers in France and other European nations also managed the lack of cotton by substituting wool and linen to manufacture clothing, instead of cotton.

Britain and France remained neutral. They would not agree to recognize the Union blockade of the Confederacy, although there was concern in the Union that Britain and France might later support the Confederacy, depending on how the Civil War progressed.

The Confederacy's tactic of withholding cotton had backfired. Just the opposite, the flow of cotton money was stopped at the time when the South most needed the money to finance the Confederate fighting. The consequences of attempting to force France and Britain to support the Confederacy haunted the South throughout the Civil War.

LESSON 24: *If people are willing to open their minds to understand the practical realities of the world, they are more likely to succeed than people who act emotionally, and hold on to their existing beliefs, not keeping their eyes open to evaluate and react when the ideas of others or unanticipated events require a change in their thinking. Being able to listen to advice from others is a key strategy for success.*

In the first year of the Civil War, Union generals were hesitant and ineffective in battle. Most civilians of the Confederate states supported the war. They secretly provided Confederate troops with food and supplies. As troops on both sides of the conflict were physically indistinguishable, the Union armies were vulnerable to attack by Southern troops using guerrilla-style warfare. It is not surprising that the Confederate troops fought ferociously, defending their lands and their way of life, using any tactics that might be successful against the Northern invaders.

Fighting a limited war in adversary territory resulted in Union defeats. The presence of Union troops doubly threatened the Southerners: their homeland and their way of life were at risk. People with their backs to the wall will fight hard.

A surprise for Lincoln early in the Civil War was that Union General George McClellan delayed engaging with the enemy troops. Although McClellan was well-regarded as an excellent organizer and had built large, well-trained armies to fight for the Union, McClellan was hesitant to commit his armies to actual fighting. He repeatedly overestimated the number of troops that his armies needed to defeat the Confederates. McClellan kept finding excuses to postpone battles and kept asking President Lincoln to assign more troops to enlarge McClellan's armies.

Part of the problem was George McClellan's attitude. He believed that a negotiated solution to the conflict with the Confederacy was possible. He personally favored a solution which would allow the Confederacy to separate from the Union. McClellan also lacked respect for President Lincoln. He did not recognize the need which President

Lincoln saw clearly: that maintaining a single, unified country was essential to the long-term security and survival of the United States.

Fortunately for the Union, the incredibly bloody battle at Antietam in 1862 was a win for the North. Before Antietam, England and France considered recognizing the Confederacy as an independent nation and giving financial support to the Confederacy, if the Confederacy appeared likely to succeed. After the South lost at Antietam, both England and France remained on the sidelines, waiting to see events unfold, not committing to what they might do. It was safer for England and France to avoid involvement, to wait and see which side was going to be the winner.

The Confederacy had counted on European support, as France had supported the Colonials in the American Revolution. But times had changed: European nations had to consider America's increased power. None of the European countries wanted to take sides until it was clear whether the Union or the Confederacy would be victorious.

The State of South Carolina had ignited the war by firing on federal Fort Sumter, despite the South not having the capacity to manufacture and produce the weapons and other necessary materials to fight a war. Not having an integrated financial system like the North, the member States of the Confederacy resisted creating a strong central financial system, as that could threaten their states' rights. Yet the Confederate government needed to raise taxes to fund the costs of fighting against the Union. Despite the urgent need for funds, Confederate leaders knew that imposing new taxes would be unpopular. They failed to take steps to raise more money.

Before the Civil War, tariffs on goods were the only taxes imposed by the States. Money to pay for the Federal government came from the Federal government's sale of western lands to settlers. Over the years, as the Civil War continued, running out of funds, the Confederacy eventually imposed income taxes, sales taxes on consumer items and an additional tax on wholesale merchants. Once imposed, however, these taxes were still inadequate to raise the amount of money required for the Confederacy to survive.

The Confederacy also sold bonds to raise additional money. Wealthy Southerners invested in their future by loaning money to their Confederate government. But when the monies from bonds were insufficient to fund the fighting, Confederate leaders made the mistake of printing excess Confederate paper money which, combined with shortages of food and goods in the South, led to massive inflation of the Confederate currency. The weakness of the Confederate finances was the greatest factor leading to the downfall of the Confederacy, which had become unable to continue a prolonged, expensive war.

The common people of the South were unhappy that the Southern Planters had exempted their own families and their overseers from military duty in the war. The Planters claimed that these exemptions from service were necessary to watch over their slaves on the plantations. In the hilly western parts of North Carolina and Virginia, which had few plantations and far fewer slaves than the wealthy areas near the east coast, people called this a "Rich Man's War."

Almost two years into the Civil War, the 1862 congressional elections in the Union went well for the Republican party. This 1862 election gave President Lincoln sufficient political support to continue to be effective as President. Lincoln, however, remained troubled over the Union's loss of battles in the South. After watching two years of bloodshed from fighting the war, Lincoln came to believe that freeing the slaves in the Confederate States might have become acceptable to the citizens of the Border states and other states in the Union. President Lincoln felt that one reason explaining why the Confederacy won battles was because the Confederacy used slave labor to do everything but fight. Southern troops traveled with slaves to cook, slaves to build fortifications, and slaves to drive supply wagons. Unlike the soldiers of the Union, all that the Confederate soldiers had to do was fight.

Two years after the fighting started, it was apparent that the Civil War might go on indefinitely. Massive destruction continued, with no end in sight. Union voters were angry at the failure of the Union armies to subdue the Confederates. Upset by the large numbers of casualties, most Union citizens were eager for the war to end.

As President and Commander in Chief of the Union military, Lincoln had the power granted by the Constitution to seize property of an adversary waging war against the Union. Lincoln stated that he had the authority to seize the slaves in the Confederacy. The ability to confiscate the adversary's slave "property" was the basis for issuing the Emancipation Proclamation to free the slaves in those adversary States which had deserted the Union to join the Confederacy.

When the war first began, Lincoln had been concerned that if he had attempted to free the Southern slaves under his war powers as President, that the Border states would immediately secede from the Union to join the Confederacy. The Border states were located just above the Mason-Dixon line, where the practice of slavery existed. The people in the Border states had been vocal that they did not want slavery to end. If the Border states had seceded from the Union and had joined the Confederacy at the beginning of the war, the Union's ability to reunite all the states in the Union would have disappeared, as the Border states would have provided so many soldiers and assets to the Confederacy that the Union could not prevent a separate nation from being created, where slavery would be allowed.

After two years of brutal fighting, Lincoln recognized that the horrific numbers of casualties had changed people's attitudes. He correctly assessed that the citizens of the Border States were just as tired of the war as were the people in the States of the North. Lincoln judged that the Border States might now accept emancipation, but only the emancipation of those slaves located within the Confederacy. Lincoln had been patient. He watched two years of bloody war before announcing the anti-slavery Emancipation Proclamation under his presidential war powers.

Lincoln had no power under the United States Constitution to free the all the slaves everywhere in the United States. That power rested in the State legislatures. If Lincoln had tried to free all the slaves when first inaugurated, the same United States Supreme Court which had enforced the Fugitive Slave Acts– requiring return of the runaway slaves --would have voided the issuance of any emancipation order from Lincoln. Only each State had the power to free its own slaves. After the Emancipation Proclamation was issued in January 1863, freeing only the slaves in the rebellious Confederacy, the Union did not free the slaves in all the States until almost two years later, when all of the States of the Union ratified the 13th Constitutional Amendment in December 1865, 8 months after the Civil war had ended.

Once word of the Emancipation Proclamation reached the slaves in the South, large numbers escaped from their masters, knowing that if they reached the Northern States, they would be free. The immediate effect of Lincoln's Proclamation was to reduce the number of slaves supporting the Southern troops.

Lincoln's gambit of emancipation had a secondary effect of convincing Britain and France to remain neutral. It was no longer politically possible for Britain or France to support a Confederate government which insisted upon continuing slavery, due to the unpopularity of slavery in these European nations. By taking high moral ground and proclaiming the emancipation of Southern slaves at the right time, Lincoln had mitigated the risk of European nations becoming involved in the war.

Emancipation immediately helped the Union. The Confederate armies lost non-combat support. Slaves escaped as soon as they saw an opportunity. In addition, emancipated slaves became fierce fighters for the Union. Emancipation strengthened the Union armies at the same time that the loss of slaves weakened the Confederate armies.

Many people in the North were upset by the Emancipation Proclamation. They felt that it would expose the North to massive immigration of Southern Black people, upsetting the structure of Northern society. Dissatisfaction with the Proclamation harmed President Lincoln's chances in the upcoming presidential election of 1864. Not surprisingly, radical Abolitionists in the North believed that immediate emancipation of all slaves should take place. The Abolitionists were not concerned with the potential for social upheaval if all the slaves in the South and North were suddenly freed. Others in the North were concerned that former slaves would take away jobs, particularly Irish and German immigrants who were already competing with each other to get work. They also feared that former slaves would racially intermingle with the whites in the North.

Lincoln believed that the majority of American voters would not accept the integration of former Black slaves. He felt that a better solution was to recolonize, to return former slaves to Africa. Black leaders were upset with Lincoln's proposed solution. Frederick Douglas argued that there was only one race of people, the human race, and that all people had their rights. Not surprisingly, very few freed slaves expressed any interest in emigrating to Africa. Most slaves had been born in America or had spent decades in America. They had no interest in starting a new life in Africa.

Lincoln and other leaders in the Republican party believed that the former slaves could operate their own free country in Africa. This solution would avoid the extreme problems of integrating former slaves into free American society. Voters in the North were concerned about the possibility of a post-emancipation "race war" igniting as freed Black people traveled north and competed for factory jobs with European immigrants.

The Union experimented with the colonization of freed slaves during the Civil War in 1863, when an entrepreneur offered the Union government to resettle five hundred freed slaves upon an island near Haiti, in the Caribbean Sea. This entrepreneur promised to establish a new colony of former American slaves by transporting them to the island and supplying them with agricultural tools, schools, and a hospital. The American government agreed to pay him to accomplish this undertaking.

The result was disaster. The entrepreneur merely dumped the freed slaves on this remote, unfamiliar island and left them with no support. Nine months later, the Union sent an American ship to rescue the survivors of the group from the island. By the time they arrived back in America, 25% of the original group of settlers had died from disease and starvation. Appalled at the outcome, neither President Lincoln nor any other American politician ever pursued recolonization further.

Turning Point: Battle at Gettysburg

Issuance of the Emancipation Proclamation by itself was not sufficient to accomplish the defeat of the Confederacy. Lincoln knew that, to win this war, Union generals had to win battles against the Confederate armies.

Ironically, it was Confederate General Robert E. Lee whose strategic choices shifted the momentum of the Civil War in favor of the Union. Lee marched his Confederate army north into Union lands, to make a surprise attack within the State of Pennsylvania. If the attack was successful in surprising the Union armies, Lee planned to advance his army to take control of Washington, D.C, the Union Capital.

After his past successes, General Lee was confident of his ability to win victory over Union armies with twice as many men as his own. In planning his attack in the North, however, Lee failed to consider that fighting against Northern armies in the North would be different from the fighting which took place in the South. The soldiers of the North would fight fiercely on their own Northern turf, to protect their own lands and their families.

If successful, Lee's planned foray into the North could have immediately ended the Civil War in the South's favor. Lee did not anticipate that the fierce battles at Gettysburg, Pennsylvania would lead to severe losses for his Confederate troops. The 3 days of fighting at Gettysburg killed or wounded more than 50,000 soldiers from both sides, with the South suffering larger numbers of casualties than the North. By the end of the third day, the Confederate armies had lost any chance to march to the Union capital in Washington. They retreated and returned to Confederate territory.

If General Lee had not led his troops to Gettysburg and instead, Lee had remained in the South, only confronting the Union troops when it was advantageous, Union voters would have seen the Civil War as a never-ending, needless waste of men and resources. If there had been no progress of Union armies after three years of fighting, the Northern voters would have voted Lincoln out of office in the upcoming presidential election of 1864. It was probable that Union voters would have then elected George McClellan to be President. McClellan had campaigned in 1864, promising that if elected, he would end the Civil War by negotiating with the Confederate leaders to agree on how to finalize the separation into two nations.

After victory at Gettysburg, Union Generals initiated a new "total war" strategy to destroy the property of the Confederate states, its purpose to deprive the Confederate armies of supplies and weapons. This new strategy also aimed to destroy Southern industry, including food production, as well as destroy all of the assets of the Planter's estates. At the same time, the Union Navy, in conjunction with the armies, began to take control of the major Southern rivers, and the Southern railroads which supplied the Confederate armies.

By this time, the Southern economy was failing. The value of the Confederate dollar had fallen dramatically due to high inflation. The Union's new "scorched earth" attacks prevented Confederate troops from obtaining adequate food, new boots, clothing, and weapons.

Despite the Union victory at Gettysburg, and General Ulysses Grant's success in driving the Confederate troops from their stronghold in Vicksburg on the Mississippi River, President Lincoln continued to lose popularity and appeared likely to lose re-election to a second term as President, as late as the summer of 1864, only a few months before the Presidential Election Day in November. Union voters had experienced too many of their soldiers dying and or returning home with severe injuries. They wanted the conflict to end. Then, a major Union victory took place: Union Admiral David Farragut won a sea battle, taking control of the last remaining Confederate port, located at Mobile Bay in Alabama. Shortly after that, Union General William Sherman's army marched through the center of Confederate manufacturing in Atlanta, Georgia, and destroyed that city. These well-publicized Union victories convinced Northern voters that the Union was going to win the war. The voters provided their support to Lincoln and re-elected him to a second term as president.

Ulysses S. Grant, known to friends as Sam Grant, started the Civil War as a nobody. Never one to seek attention, he focused on doing his job as a soldier. Through luck and hard work, he rose to the rank of General in the Union Army, then became lead General, and in later years, became President of the United States. It is safe to say that it is more likely than not that the South would have won the Civil War if there had been no General Grant, or at least, someone who had Grant's practical intelligence and tenacity.

ULYSSES S. GRANT
(Image from The Smithsonian)

Grant's success is a testament to the American values of integrity and honesty. He lived by these American ideals and proved their effectiveness. He also had the benefit of being naturally courageous. His goal in fighting was to get as close as possible to opposing armies, and then battle relentlessly to win the fight.

Grant's greatest concern was that a commander who did not agree with his strategies would prevent him from engaging in battle. Superior officers sometimes criticized Grant for going too far, for attacking when he had insufficient authority. Grant believed that victory finally came after exhaustion affected both sides. By pushing to fight beyond exhaustion, one side would win.

Yet Grant was humane. Coming upon a Union soldier and a Confederate soldier, lying on the ground together, both severely wounded, Grant dismounted from his horse and asked one of his officers for a flask. Grant gave each soldier a drink of brandy. When the ambulance wagon arrived, Grant ordered that both soldiers go to the hospital in the same wagon. He said: "Take them both together; the war is over between them."

Grant used few words and had no interest in putting on a show. Calm and quiet, he was unusually modest. Grant never looked to be the center of attention, although he did insist upon riding his horse at the front of his army when it traveled. Throughout his career, people were surprised to learn that this unassuming man was somebody important.

Grant paid little attention to his appearance. His clothing, haircut and beard tended to be unkempt. Close friends knew him to be a talker, but if there was anyone around that Grant did not know or trust, he became a man of few words. He almost never gave speeches, and never spoke at length to the troops he commanded. When Grant did say something, his subordinates paid attention. He worked carefully and quietly, attending to detail. For instance, Grant always made sure that all of his troops received their mail promptly and predictably. He knew what it meant to his soldiers to have contact and emotional support from home.

Well-schooled in the technical details of waging war, Grant was diligent in reviewing plans and looking at maps. He developed ideas about novel steps to defeat the other side. He tirelessly made plans and wrote orders to his subordinates, working late into the night. Not preoccupied with politics or personalities, he focused on winning victory.

Grant was scrupulously honest. When his father asked Grant to meet with friends of his father to help get them government contracts for work or jobs, Grant refused. He operated without any partiality, favor, or affection for or to anyone. He had strength of character. If there were a problem, Grant would tell the truth about what happened. He took whatever blame was due to him.

One weakness haunted him: as a young soldier, when he was lonely, he tended to drink too much. This got him a bad reputation. His reputation for drinking hurt him as he rose through the military ranks. He did not drink when there was work to do, or when his wife and children were with him. Receiving promotions and weighed down with additional responsibilities, Grant's alcohol abuse stopped.

After newspapers reported Grant's military successes, he became famous as "Unconditional Surrender" Grant, from his insistence that defeated Southern generals capitulate without any conditions, or the fighting would not stop. Grant wrote about why aggressive fighting and moving quickly was the best way to save lives:

"I want to push on as rapidly as possible to save hard fighting. These terrible battles are very good things to read about for persons who lose no friends, but I am decidedly in favor of having as little of it as possible. The way to avoid it is to push forward as vigorously as possible."

Grant believed that when opposing armies were at a stalemate, the army which boldly made one more attack was the army which was likely to win. Sometimes, Grant was more optimistic than proved to be realistic, but on the whole, his willingness to fight made him successful in most battles, far more successful than other Union Generals who preceded him.

Grant's ability to encourage his troops to keep fighting, and his ability to project optimism set him apart from his peers. Even when there were bad days for his armies, Grant was stubbornly optimistic that the next day would bring victory.

At the same time, he was sensitive to criticism, which is not surprising as he was very conscientious. He wrote the following letter to his sister about criticism against him in the newspapers:

"...(T)here are an immense number of lives staked upon my judgment and acts. I am extended now like a peninsula into enemy country, with a large army depending for their daily bread upon keeping open a line of railroad running one hundred and ninety miles through an enemy's, or, at least, through territory occupied by a people terribly embittered and hostile to us. With all this I suffer the mortification of seeing myself attacked right and left by people at home professing patriotism and love of country, who never heard the whistle of a hostile bullet...I am thankful, however that, although such people make a great noise, the masses are not like them."

Other Union Generals could be unfair to Grant, to make him look bad; they were quick to take credit due to him and, at the same time, criticize him to enhance their own power and prevent Grant from receiving the positive recognition he deserved. The influence of President Lincoln helped Grant to overcome these personal attacks. Lincoln repeatedly promoted him, recognizing that Grant kept winning battles and kept pursuing the enemy.

One of the problems for Union armies fighting in the South was an illegal market for cotton: rather than burn their unsaleable cotton, Planters made deals with traders from the North to sell cotton, the prices having risen further due to the war. At the same time, the South was short of all types of items, including salt, which was essential to preserving meat to feed the Southern soldiers. This salt shortage created an incentive for the Planters to sell cotton to their enemies in the North to get money to pay for salt and for other food to feed Confederate soldiers. American political leaders in Washington, DC, actually encouraged this trade. Union General Sherman complained that the money received in the South from the sale of cotton allowed the Confederacy to purchase weapons and ammunition to kill Union soldiers.

People high up in the Union government profited from this trading. Grant did everything possible to stop it, even though Grant's father and his father's business associates encouraged this trading, and made it look like Grant was supporting the trading. Grant refused to cooperate with his father's schemes. He would not permit profits from government work to go to anyone connected with the Grant family.

Grant assigned working groups of newly freed slaves from the South to harvest the cotton which was sitting in the fields. He organized former slaves into fighting units. Through fighting for the Union, they could gain their citizenship and have the right to vote. His humility, humanity and practical common sense allowed Grant to find solutions that other Northern leaders overlooked.

More than one newspaper writer described General Grant as modest and honest, even-tempered, and wise. He was a sincere, thoughtful, unaffected, unpretending hero, a friendly man but not sentimental. Other writers noted that Grant said and did as little as possible in front of his men, which his men appreciated. There was no show, no pomp. He wore a plain uniform. New soldiers, seeing Grant, could not believe that he had the title of Commanding General. He was a teammate as well as a leader. His soldiers believed in him.

Grant also had the ability to defuse conflicts within his troops. When there were arguments among his men, Grant could find a way to work things out, quickly and quietly. His officers followed his orders without complaint.

Grant tried to write all of his own Orders, rather than explain to a subordinate what to write. Grant retained minute details about situations, and intimately knew the men and weaponry in his armies. His abilities improved as the war continued. With the Confederate armies weakened, Grant understood precisely the actions needed to win.

Rumors of Grant's alcoholism continued, but President Lincoln put an end to them, famously stating that Lincoln wanted to find out what brand of whiskey Grant drank, because if it should make Union generals fight like Grant, Lincoln would like to get some of that whiskey and distribute it to the other generals.

Grant believed that the Confederate rebellion could only terminate by complete subjugation of the South. It was the duty of the armies of the North to use every means to weaken the enemy, by destroying their subsistence, withdrawing their means of cultivating their fields, and preventing them from resupplying in every way possible. The Union strategy impaired the Confederate ability to fight, through depletion of Southern resources. At the same time, Grant ordered freed southern Black men to fight in Union regiments, which they were glad to do. Grant ordered his existing troops to welcome, feed, clothe, and arm these additional fighters.

Grant's decisive victory at Vicksburg gave the Union control of the Mississippi River. After the Confederacy lost in battle at Vicksburg, the Union troops mingled with their Confederate adversaries, and refrained from cheering, saddened at seeing the dejection of their former antagonists. There was a feeling of understanding, a brotherhood which developed between the former fighters. The move towards peace was a move towards fellowship.

Union General Sherman's victories soon followed Grant's victory, with Sherman's army destroying everything—railroads, factories, bridges, military supplies, buildings, farms, homes, and food-- diagonally across Georgia, marching in a 60-mile-wide swath from northwest to southeast. The assets of the South, including plantations, farms, and factories were the targets of the Union armies.

Grant was willing to drive every family out of whole counties. After defeating one of the Southern armies, Grant wrote:

"The (Southern) men had behaved so well that I did not want to humiliate them. I believed that consideration for their feelings would make them less dangerous foes during the continuation of hostilities and better citizens after the war was over."

When the Union armies won battles, Grant paroled Confederate soldiers if they swore not to fight again against the Union troops. Confederate generals had no way to stop their soldiers from going home, as most soldiers were tired of fighting and wanted to see their families. Grant continued to win battles and was losing fewer of his own soldiers.

Surprisingly, General Grant and General Sherman both detested the destruction of war, but each had learned that insufficient aggression only lengthens wars. Prolonged fighting creates a greater loss of life. If the Union had undertaken the tactic of "scorched earth" aggression from the beginning of the war, the fighting would have been over sooner, with far fewer injuries and deaths.

LESSON 25: *Uncertainty about how a conflict will proceed should be the prime motivator for parties to settle disputes by agreement, rather than take on the risks of fighting.*

Before engaging in the Civil war, both sides had predicted a short war. The opposite was true: the Civil war was lengthy, the most violent and bloody conflict in American history. If meaningful settlement discussions had taken place before the South seceded, Southern leaders might have recognized the possible downsides of secession before they decided that secession was their only course of action.

Leaders frequently fail due to irrational belief in a positive outcome. These leaders prohibit debate. They claim disloyalty of anyone expressing doubt or concern about entering into a war. No one may question or criticize them. There is a considerable advantage to leaders who are open-minded, rational, and have the ability to put aside ego and emotion. The personalities and abilities of the leaders are part of the "luck" which can change the course of wars. It was partly through luck and chance that people like President Lincoln and General Grant both rose to the heights of power for the Union. Different outcomes might have been obtained had different leaders been in charge.

When already engaged in a war, leaders may rely upon unfounded assumptions, not recognizing that continuing the fight is not likely to give them what they want and that continuing to battle will leave them and their people worse off. Only irrational leaders fight when they should know that losing is inevitable. Rational leaders face defeat by intelligently moving forward to negotiate the best settlement for their side. Even worse are the leaders who believe that they would rather die than reach an agreement.

JEFFERSON DAVIS
(Image from The Smithsonian)

Intelligent and knowledgeable about fighting wars, Confederate President Jefferson Davis had been a United States senator and Secretary of War before the Civil war. As a young man, he had survived difficult events: While a cadet at West Point, he drank heavily at a party, fell off a cliff, and suffered serious multiple broken bones and permanently impaired vision in one eye. While a young man, Davis, and his new bride both contracted the disease Malaria. She died from the disease only three months after they were married. Post-malarial fevers plagued Davis throughout his life.

He was not charismatic. Although well-liked by his friends, and proficient as a politician, Davis was aloof, with a cold personality. When Confederate women rioted over rises in prices of food in 1863, Davis threatened to have troops fire upon these Southern women if they failed to disperse. He was a rigid thinker, insensitive to the opinions of others. He believed that it was better to die trying to retain the Southern plantation way of life, than live in a world without the prosperity and control to which the Planters had been accustomed.

Delegating responsibility to others in the Confederate government was difficult for him. Davis spent too much time involved in detailed military discussions instead of entrusting the fighting to his generals. A secondary problem was Davis's reluctance, when events demanded, to remove his friends from positions of power.

The way in which Confederate politics worked created additional problems for the South. There was no two-party system in the Confederacy. Southern leaders believed that two-party politics led to selfish decision-making, that the dissent inherent in the two-party system undermined good government. The problem created by the South's single-party politics was the lack of a mechanism for criticism of bad decisions. Dissent would have enabled arguments in favor of increasing taxes to support the value of Confederate money. Inflation caused Southern soldiers to desert from the military to assist their families' survival. Allowing dissent would have allowed arguments in favor of drafting Confederate soldiers earlier. The failure to have a two-party system inhibited adaptation to the changing needs of the South. Unattended financial problems of the Confederacy grew and later destroyed the Confederate ability to maintain adequate food, clothing, and weaponry for its soldiers.

Jefferson Davis was not the type to push the Southern Confederate Congress to do the necessary, most importantly to raise taxes to pay for fighting the war. Pre-war prosperity had spoiled Southern leaders. They clung to old ways of thinking. Southern people who owned slaves were in the great minority. Southerners who did not own slaves grew resentful of the extent to which war affected their lives.

The Confederate Congress insisted upon meeting in secret session. They did not see any need to inform the Confederate public about what they were doing. There were no records kept of votes and decision-making. Southern leaders abused alcohol, quarreled, and resorted to violence while in session with each other. Confederate leaders who lived far from the Confederate capital in Richmond, Virginia, frequently missed important debates and discussions.

Younger Southern leaders had pursued wealth by creating new plantations in the West, which required the extension of slavery to new states and territories. They would not admit that slavery needed to end. They refused to take steps to negotiate for the best economic deal to end slavery gradually. Instead, blinded by greed and self-interest, they foolishly proceeded upon a dangerous path which led to catastrophe for their side.

LESSON 26: *It is never good to risk everything if you do not have to. It is always better to negotiate to obtain a known outcome you can live with, rather than to fight and receive an outcome far worse. This is especially true when things keep going wrong for your side.*

Complete mobilization of the people of the South was necessary to fight the war, but the Confederate Congress wanted to stand firm on principles of states' rights and individual freedom, at a time when it was essential to adapt and accept burdensome temporary measures, such as requiring military service, paying higher taxes and temporary loss of individual rights. The Confederacy needed flexibility in the short term to survive. The Confederate leaders' refusal to undertake necessary temporary measures resulted in the deterioration of civilian living conditions. Moreover, Confederate troops lacked the supplies needed to resist invasion from the armies of the North.

Lack of money impaired Confederate fighters. Improvements in modern weaponry gave the Union an advantage over the Confederacy in the last two years of the Civil War. Breech-loading rifles and repeating rifles superseded single shot muskets. The rifles could fire seven shots without reloading. These improved weapons, which the Confederacy could not afford, gave the advantage to the Union troops. The barrels of these new rifles had grooves which made the bullets to spin at a high rate of speed, stabilizing their trajectories in the same way that American footballs spin, making them stable and improving accuracy.

These new rifles increased the accuracy of the Union shooters, particularly over long distances. Confederate troops used older muskets with no grooves in the barrels. The round musket balls shot by Confederate fighters were much less effective than Northern bullets. The balls quickly lost accuracy and speed as they traveled over distance. More importantly, Confederate soldiers using muskets took more time and effort to reload after each shot. Southern shooters were unable to counter the rapid fire of Union troops. The South's failure to have sufficient monies to purchase accurate repeating rifles is a good example of circumstances which Confederate leaders could not have foreseen as they optimistically set out to form their own nation years before.

Lack of sufficient funds also resulted in poor maintenance of the Confederacy's network of railroads. Broken railroads prevented needed supplies from reaching Confederate troops. Meanwhile, the Union armies repaired their railroads quickly, and had few supply problems. The destruction of Southern plantations, factories and railroads impaired the Confederacy's operations. Confederate soldiers grew thin and worn out, although most remained surprisingly strong fighters.

As the balance in the Civil War tilted in favor of the Union, Confederate families had difficulty obtaining necessities for life, including shelter and clothing. Many only had food for one or two meals per day. There was no coffee. Paper was a rare commodity. The earnings of working people in the South were less than half of what they had earned before the war started. Southerners complained that they were worse off now than they had been under the Union government.

In the last year of the Civil War, Confederate soldiers deserted in greater numbers, often returning home to assist their desperate families. Many wives and children lost their homes and became refugees, traveling far away from home to find food and shelter. As more families traveled, other communities did not welcome them, simply because there was not enough to go around.

Severe inflation devalued Confederate money. In effect, towards the end of the Civil War, the Confederate soldiers were fighting without pay. Taxing the people to obtain more Confederate dollars did not make sense to Confederate leaders as Confederate dollars now held little value. Dire circumstances forced Confederate leaders to collect taxes in the form of produce and goods, at a percentage of 10% of whatever its citizens possessed. This flat tax hurt the smaller farmers and merchants. They needed every penny to get by. Taking 10 percent away from the Planters made a small difference to them, as the planters retained more than sufficient money to pay for the necessities of life.

The Confederate government had confiscated horses and other necessary items from its citizens since the beginning of the Civil War, but the receipts given to citizens for confiscated property were payable in Confederate dollars, which had become worthless. The Confederate choices disadvantaged their own people. What was the point of fighting if fighting destroyed their lives?

Conditions became so bad in the South that the Confederate leaders finally started drafting soldiers to fight in the armies. Southerners saw the draft as a threat to the freedoms which they had fought to preserve. Towards the end of the Civil War, Southern leaders even drafted slaves to fight as Confederate soldiers, which upset the white people of the South. The Confederate messaging at the beginning of the war had been that the South would never allow slaves to fight, for fear of providing access to firearms which could support a Black insurrection.

Southern women and children jammed trains, running away from the fighting, subject to harassment and interference by Union troops. Even worse, Southern deserters and Southern criminal "bushwhackers" preyed on their own people, stealing property, and committing the worst sorts of brutalities.

Southern speculators found ways to make money out of the chaos. Refugees lost everything they had ever owned. Southern society unraveled as Union fighters proceeded, devastating the South, destroying houses, animals, crops, and anything of value within reach of the Union armies.

The greatest tragedies occur when a side that is likely to lose cannot or will not recognize defeat is inevitable. The best strategy under those circumstances is to concede under the best terms available by making an agreement to settle the fight, to stop being enemies, and if possible, to set the table to work together in the future. Jefferson Davis refused to admit Confederate defeat more than a year before the war ended. His belief that fighting must continue was irrational and emotional. Catastrophe is never preferable to settlement. Continuing the fight gave leaders of the South a far worse outcome than they could ever have anticipated.

Abolitionist leaders in the North had argued that, once the Civil War ended, the lands of the Confederate soldiers should be confiscated, divided into parcels, and be given to freed slaves. Abolitionists argued for harsh punishment of the Confederate leaders, including the destruction of the plantations. The Abolitionists wanted to completely transform the South.

When General Lee's Confederate army finally surrendered to General Grant's army at the small hamlet known as Appomattox Courthouse, Northern politicians demanded that the Union soldiers arrest or kill the Southern traitors who had fought against the Union.

Having already discussed with President Lincoln the best way to reunite the Union, when General Lee surrendered his Southern army, Union General Grant ordered that all Confederate soldiers could return to their homes, so long as they laid down their weapons, and promised never to fight against the Union again. Grant also allowed Southern soldiers to keep their horses so that they could start farming as soon as they returned to their homes.

President Lincoln wanted the former rebels to accept conquest by the Union. If the South did not accept conquest, the North would need to maintain large military forces in the South, risking terrorist attacks from former rebels. Lincoln knew that being gentle with the Confederates was the best pathway toward lasting peace. He believed Southern people were more likely to accept gradual change. Harsh punishment and attempts to dramatically remake the Southern states would cause resistance to their joining the Union. Lincoln understood that instituting harsh measures, despite good intentions, might lead to an American counter-revolution and "race-war," fomented by the dispossessed former leaders of the South.

The outcome of any war may be determined in favor of the side with greater power, but other factors need consideration: the winning side usually takes charge of the loser's people and property. What happens next depends on the performance of the leaders of the winning side. Will they be able to retain the gains of war? Will the winners be able to control the people of the nation they defeated? All sides suffer in a war, but one side must have believed fighting was worth it, or that side would not have proceeded to fight. Too often, wars turn out to be a waste.

In most other wars in history before that time, rebels were either executed or put into prison, their lands and property confiscated in punishment. Lincoln determined that the United States needed healing after the war ended. The Union did as much as possible to welcome the return of the Southern States to the Union. The United States would be at its strongest when all its people unified, to the extent possible. Lincoln's philosophy of forgiveness helped to reduce bad feelings, but nothing could eliminate Southern resentment of the North's devastation of the Confederate lands.

Lincoln's assassination took place only 10 days after the surrender of Lee's Confederate army to General Grant. The unfortunate assassination plot, undertaken by a small group of Southern zealots, almost derailed the North's plans to welcome the return of the Southern states. Politicians in the North initially believed that Confederate leaders had ordered the assassination. These Northern politicians demanded that severe punishments to the Confederate leaders should follow. The majority in the North decided against severe punishment, which was appropriate, as post-war investigations showed that John Wilkes Booth and his associates carried out the assassination of Lincoln and that unsuccessful assassination attempt on the life of Secretary of State Seward without knowledge or approval from Southern leaders.

Reviewing where things stood when the Civil War ended 4 years after it had started, there is no doubt that the Civil War had brought disaster to the South. This terrible war accomplished absolutely nothing that the Southern leaders had intended. In fact, the Civil War ended the Planter way of life to a much greater extent than if both sides reached a pre-war negotiated solution to end slavery. More than 250,000 Confederate soldiers died in the Civil War. It is likely that the deaths of Southern civilians were greater. There are no reliable records of civilian deaths in the South.

In retrospect, once the Civil War started, the Union generals needed to fight aggressively to be able to crush the Confederate armies. Half-hearted fighting had no positive effect in bringing resolution. Stalemate increased the extent of destruction. When the Northern generals and their armies finally undertook the strategy of completely destroying the South's food, transportation, manufacturing and property, these actions moved the war forward to Northern victory.

When the war began, no one knew how effective Abraham Lincoln would be as President. The South had a strong hand to play before the war. If years earlier, the voters in the Northern states and the Border states had accepted Lincoln's proposal that the Union government buy the slaves their freedom, both sides could have obtained a negotiated settlement before any fighting started, the costs of war and loss of lives averted. When the war began, leaders in the North and South had been overly optimistic that the war would rapidly resolve in their favor.

The leaders of the South had viewed any attempt to end or restrict slavery as intolerable. They were willing to fight to the death to preserve their way of life. An emotional, almost religious zeal in favor of the slave system caused Southern leaders to underestimate their downside. The Southern leaders failed to recognize the limits of their power. Better perception of their vulnerabilities could have led to negotiation with the North to achieve a deal preserving Southern infrastructure and Southern lives, even though the South would have to make significant changes in their way of living as slavery faded away.

Given the fixed attitudes of the Southern leaders, there was no way to settle the Civil War in advance of the war starting. It was only when the Southern leaders ran out of options that they were willing to stop fighting. Rigidly holding on to an unlikely chance of success, when faced with imminent destruction, was short-sighted. Even when their infrastructure was crumbling, Confederate leaders convinced themselves that the fighting must continue. Overestimating their superiority and the likelihood of positive results led to disaster for the Southern leaders.

There was one good outcome from the Civil War: Lincoln's adept handling of the Emancipation Proclamation resulted in a much earlier end to slavery.

After the war ended, historians calculated the mathematical odds of a soldier dying in the Civil War, both for Union and Confederate soldiers. There had been a 6% chance of a soldier dying from wounds or fighting, and an additional 10% chance of death from disease or accident. So altogether, the average chances of any soldier dying in the Civil War were 16%, or about one chance in six. These are the same odds as dying from playing Russian Roulette with a 6-cylinder revolver, an activity which most rational people would avoid. If the Southern leaders had understood their true potential for loss, they could have made better choices for themselves and their people.

Prior to the Civil War, settlement discussions had been fruitless. If the Southern leaders had accurately assessed the risks they faced, it is likely that the Civil War would have ended sooner, with less destruction, and with less bad feelings. By continuing to fight even when the loss was inevitable, the Southern leaders exacerbated their losses much more than was necessary. They had gained nothing positive after suffering four terrible years. Closed minds and unwillingness to negotiate led to the devastation of the South.

PART 4: The Vietnam War—

A Study in Hubris

"I've got a wife, a kid, another on the way
I might get home if I can live through today
Before I came out here I never used to pray
Nobody loves me here
Nobody loves me here."

– From the song "Dad's Gonna Kill Me,"
by Richard Thompson

Looking at the years from 1919 until 1941, the period between World War I and America's entry into World War II, American foreign policy avoided entanglement in the wars and conflicts between other nations. The devastating Japanese attack upon the American fleet of warships stationed at Pearl Harbor, Hawaii, in 1941 ended America's isolation. This surprise Japanese attack revealed the embarrassing unpreparedness of the American military. American voters questioned the competency of their military leaders.

America responded aggressively to the Japanese attacks in the Pacific, while, at the same time, Americans fought against the Nazis in Europe eventually obtaining victories against both Germany and Japan in 1945. The American people were pleased with the success of their reinvigorated military. Isolationism had proved to be an ineffective strategy. Political unity within America had developed in response to the threats from German Nazis and the Japanese forces. Most Americans had learned that America must actively engage around the world, to protect America and its interests.

When World War II ended in 1945, a new threat of war from Russian communists became a real possibility. American leaders were concerned about the spread of communism from Russia to the governments of other nations. American leaders believed that the spread of communism threatened America and other nations around the world. It appeared that communists might seize power in any other nation, should America fail to act. These American leaders embraced active intervention in the affairs of other nations to prevent the spread of communism from destroying the entire capitalist financial system of the world.

Communist leaders in Russia held great power over their people, governing through secret processes. Under communism, there was no two-party system to allow citizens to criticize when they thought that their government had acted unwisely. Communist leaders promised that they would do what was best for their people. The history of communist governments in the first half of the 20th century confirms that there has been little individual freedom in Russia since the Russian Revolution created the first communist-controlled government in 1917.

Fear of communism arose in Europe and America, due to the rise of communist nations after World War II. Russia's communist government had come to power only 30 years before the end of World War II. The world's most populous nation, China underwent a civil war between capitalists and communists following the Japanese surrender in 1945. The civil war in China ended four years later, in 1949, when communist leader Mao Zedong defeated capitalist leader Chang Kai Shek. This new Chinese communist government controlled all of China by 1950. Western leaders feared that communism would spread within nearby Southeast Asia. With communist governments now controlling both Russia and China, Monarchs and leaders of democratic nations around the globe wondered if the spread of communism would destroy their systems of government.

After World War II ended, American leaders revealed that communists had placed spies in the American nuclear weapons program, obtaining access to top-secret scientific documents. This theft of American technology enabled Russia to quickly develop its own nuclear bomb capability. It is understandable that the American leaders were anxious about the threat of conflicts with the leaders of Russia and China, who held strong beliefs that communism would soon eclipse capitalism.

Congression investigations revealed that communists had secretly infiltrated the American government decades before, in the 1930s. The extent of the infiltration of communists was unknown. Russia's post-World War II power enabled it to create the Soviet Union, transitioning from being an ally to becoming an enemy of America. This was the time of the "Red Scare" in the United States, the term referring to the red flags of communist-controlled Russia and China. Undercover communist agents had achieved high-level jobs in the American government. American leaders took extreme measures to root out the communists. Americans also feared that a nuclear war with Russia was on the verge of erupting.

Under communism, the rights of the citizens as a group are superior to the rights of any individual. Communist leaders proclaimed that the workers and the farmers were the beneficiaries of their communist systems, enriched by the elimination of wealthy capitalists in those nations.

Understanding the differences between capitalism and communism is fundamental to understanding the causes of the war in Vietnam. Compared to the strict control of citizens by communist governments, democratic governments allow their citizens freedom of speech to express differences in opinion. People can express varying degrees of feedback and criticism about their governments, the extent depending upon the laws of the particular capitalist nation. Leaders in capitalist countries compete with each other for votes, and the winners are elected to lead for specified terms of office. Capitalism typically grows strong economies, encourages invention and innovation, and attracts immigrants looking for opportunity and a better life. A multi-party capitalist system encourages transparency of government decision-making and the free exchange of ideas and provides the opportunity for people in the minority to argue for better solutions.

When citizens have the power to choose new leaders if they are unhappy with their current leadership, they usually choose leaders who better serve their needs. The American Constitution provides its citizens with the freedom to make choices about their own future. People who act in their own interests, following the incentives provided by capitalism, are the foundation of prosperity in America.

Individuals are much less free under communism. There is no right to privacy. Communist governments discourage and punish dissenting speech and the practice of religion. Every neighborhood has residents who secretly inform when any person speaks unfavorably about the government. Criticism of a communist government brings punishment. Communist leaders believe that they know what is best for their people. Ordinary citizens have no right to free elections, have no right to replace current leaders under any circumstances, despite most communist governments claiming that they have free elections.

Once communists gain control of a nation, the new communist government confiscates all private property and land from its citizens, giving the leaders of the communist government power to control all property and businesses for the good of the people. Communist leaders decide which goods and services the people need, typically

143

controlling all manufacturing, all farming, and all jobs. The government owns all the stores and decides what the stores will sell. There is no free marketplace, except that underground economies usually develop to help people obtain items they want, when their government is not making those items available.

History has revealed that the weakness of communist governments is that they lack accountability to their people, as communist government decision-making is opaque. There is little opportunity for effective dissent. Communist leaders do not look to their citizens for guidance, nor do communist governments easily make changes. Communist economies have not provided quality goods and services for their people, compared to the goods and services capitalism provides.

The term "Cold War" refers to the post-World War II conflict between America and the Soviet Union, which included Russia and smaller nations surrounding Russia, all under the control of a federal Soviet communist government. There was no direct fighting between the armies of America and the Soviet Union during the Cold War. Instead, a series of "proxy wars" arose in different regions of the world. America supported nations with capitalist governments, while the Soviets supported nations with communist governments, with other governments throughout the world becoming allies to one of the two superpowers.

By 1950, their leaders told Americans that the spread of communism was now the greatest threat to America. Focused on the omnipresent threat of nuclear war, American voters did not object to supporting capitalist countries throughout the world to prevent the further spread of communism.

American corporations profited from making business deals around the world in the post-World War II economic boom. The corporations were concerned that the spread of communism would limit beneficial trade expansion, threatening their profits. Corporate lobbying and financial support of political campaigns in America encouraged American leaders to expand American trade around the world to benefit American businesses.

Although there was only minimal governmental assistance to America's poor and needy before World War II, substantial assistance of the poor and needy came from private charities, primarily operated by religious organizations, although the American government had created a limited safety net before World War II, with the passage of the Social Security Act.

Communist leaders in Russia and China were able to take power by convincing people that capitalism was an uncaring system, where the powerful wealthy exploited and took advantage of the workers and the poor. Ironically, after World War II, in response to the criticism of lack of caring, and in response to the requests of voters, the governments of America and the rest of the Western world created additional social programs and safety nets, which did not exist before.

JOHN FOSTER DULLES
(Image from the Library of Congress)

Following World War II, American Secretary of State and international power broker, John Foster Dulles was personally responsible for several secret American interventions in other nations around the globe. He championed the extension of American capitalism worldwide, without reservation. It is likely that America would not have become entangled in Vietnam but for Dulles' power and influence. His grandfather, John Watson

Foster, an American Secretary of State of the prior generation, had helped to overthrow Queen Liliuokalani of Hawaii in 1893, and made Hawaii a territory of the United States, later to become the 50th state. The Dulles family was the product of a Presbyterian upbringing. They operated with a capitalist missionary ethos, believing that America's success depended upon American businesses developing trade relationships with other nations on America's terms.

Before becoming Secretary of State, John Foster Dulles had practiced law as a member of the prestigious New York law firm Sullivan & Cromwell, where he worked on behalf of American corporations internationally. John Foster Dulles believed that whatever benefitted American business also benefitted the world as a whole. His grandfather's influence and advice had helped him make foreign connections.

Before World War II, John Foster Dulles' representation of American banks generated large profits from increases in international trade. His influence applied political pressure upon foreign countries to do business in the manner that America wanted. He held a rigid perspective: whatever helped his clients was good. His zeal clouded his judgment to the extent that he claimed in 1939 that Germany, Italy, and Japan would not engage in aggression against the United States, when exactly the opposite was true. Shortly after Dulles' pronouncements that America should support the Nazi governments in Germany, Mussolini's fascist Italy, and the government of Japan, then controlled by religiously fanatical leaders, all three nations became active combatants against America in World War II.

John Foster Dulles had always been strongly anti-communist. Along with other advisors to American President Harry Truman after World War II, Dulles preached that Soviet communism was part of a global communist conspiracy whose goal was to destroy freedom and eliminate the West. Dulles saw America's relationship with communist governments as a conflict of "black and white, them vs. us." Under Dulles' influence, President Truman spoke in support of what was later known as the Truman Doctrine, that civilization itself was at risk from communism. President Truman declared that America would fight against the advance of communism anywhere in the world. He was convinced that saving the world and capitalistic civilization from communism justified American involvement.

Republican President Eisenhower appointed John Foster Dulles Secretary of State, after democratic president Harry Truman failed re-election as president. Working together with his brother Allen Dulles, then Director of the Central Intelligence Agency (CIA), they were behind aggressive covert American interventions in foreign governments, which they believed were unfriendly to America or whose governments they believed might turn to communism.

Even though President Eisenhower had wanted to end American involvement in the Korean War of 1950-1953, Dulles advised Eisenhower to keep fighting in Korea in order to confront China, which was supporting the Korean communists. Dulles' purpose was to create fear of the United States in Chinese leaders. President Eisenhower disregarded John Foster Dulles' advice and ordered an end to the Korean War, although President Eisenhower later approved secret actions by the American Central Intelligence Agency (CIA) to interfere with governments of other nations believed to be unfriendly to American interests. Pursuing secret agendas against foreign governments risked harming America's reputation for integrity. It was unwise for American leaders to deny that they were interfering with other nations, at the same time that America's CIA was secretly involved in attempts to manipulate and politically control activities inside other nations.

John Foster Dulles promoted the "Domino Theory," that any change which established communism in one nation would have the effect of seeding communist takeovers in more nations, just as what happens when the first domino starts a line of other dominos falling. Although John Foster Dulles had indicated to the press that America would not intervene in the governments of other nations, he secretly engaged in extensive efforts to influence the governments and politics of nations around the world, in order to support America and American businesses.

The Dulles brothers engineered the overthrow of Iran's leader, Mohammad Mossadegh, placing American-friendly Reza Pahlavi as Shah of Iran in 1953. The CIA helped topple the government of Guatemala in 1954, which benefitted America's United Fruit Company, (today known as "Chiquita.") The Dulles later masterminded a plan for covert political intervention in Indonesia in 1958, which failed, as did their attempts to change the political leaders in Egypt and the Congo.

After John Foster Dulles died in 1959, his brother Allen Dulles later masterminded the unsuccessful American Bay of Pigs invasion of Cuba in 1961. This ill-advised American aggression motivated the Cuban communists under Fidel Castro to hatch a plan with the Soviet government to place nuclear missiles in Cuba, aimed at America, less than one hundred miles away. The discovery of the nuclear missile threat to America led to the Cuban Missile Crisis in 1962, which brought America to the edge of fighting a nuclear war. Realizing that America was planning to attack Cuba with weapons of mass destruction, the Soviet Union dismantled and removed the missile sites from Cuba.

The Dulles brothers were unconcerned that they interfered with the opportunities of citizens of other nations to be self-governing. The Dulles believed other nations' pursuit of independence and nationalism was sufficient to justify American interference. Preventing communist political victories was all the justification needed for

America to undertake covert action to manipulate the politics within those nations.

The Dulles brothers acted to enhance profitability for American corporations at the expense of weaker nations. Although they strongly believed they were acting in America's interests, the Dulles brothers' covert involvement backfired, hurting America's image around the world. Prime Minister of Britain and an astute observer, Winston Churchill, described John Foster Dulles as a rare "a bull who carries his own china shop around with him."

The Dulles brothers and other American leaders did not hesitate to involve America in Vietnam to try to prevent communism from taking hold in that nation. It is important to briefly explore Vietnam's history to understand how American troops came to fight in Vietnam.

Chinese rulers had conquered Vietnam, on and off, for more than one thousand years before the 20th century. During the few times when the Chinese empire was not in control of Vietnam, warlords within Vietnam competed for control.

European colonial rule of Vietnam began in 1883, when 20,000 French troops invaded, with the goal of making Vietnam into a colony for France. At this same time, France and other European nations competed to establish and retain colonies in Africa, Asia, the Caribbean and South America, all seeking the economic advantages and profits from controlling and exploiting the natural resources of weaker nations.

After taking control of Vietnam in 1883, the French created a planter's economy in Vietnam, not unlike the planter's economy of the American South prior to the American Civil War. The French cruelly exploited the Vietnamese people, transplanting the French language and French culture into Vietnam. Saigon became known as the "Paris of the East." French immigrants to Vietnam rarely mixed with the

Vietnamese people, whom the French treated as second-class citizens in their own country.

French leaders in Vietnam encouraged the use of opium and alcohol to help maintain their control of the local population. French military strength controlled all of Vietnam for 57 years, until 1940, when the militaristic government of Japan conquered Vietnam. The Japanese military dominated much of Southeast Asia before and during World War II. At the same time, Hitler's German army invaded France, forcing the French forces in Vietnam to return to Europe to try to save France.

The Japanese invaders brutally mistreated the Vietnamese people, using the same tactics that the Japanese had used to dominate other Southeast Asian countries. On Japan's watch, drought and the resulting famine starved and ended the lives of more than one million Vietnamese people. The United States eventually conquered Japan at the end of World War II in 1945. Afterward, the French military returned to Vietnam to maintain Vietnam as a French colony.

The politics within Vietnam changed following World War II. Backed by money and weapons supplied by the communist Russian and Chinese governments, Vietnamese fighters attempted to take control of Vietnam. Ironically, despite their own nation having just been freed from subjugation to Nazi Germany, the French were determined to maintain control of the people of Vietnam, despite comments from the leaders of other European nations that it was unwise for the French to return to Vietnam, due to Vietnam's powerful desire for independence.

It is not surprising that the Vietnamese people were unhappy about the return of the French. Through decades of international networking before World War II, Vietnamese leader Ho Chi Minh had become a beacon for freedom for the Vietnamese people. He tirelessly traveled the world seeking support for a free Vietnam since the 1920s. Ho Chi

Minh argued for communist control of Vietnam, as he believed that a communist government system would provide the best future for an independent Vietnam to govern itself. Ho Chi Minh was charismatic and lived sparely, like a peasant. People called him "Uncle Ho." He supported the interests of the Vietnamese people. As Ho Chi Minh was a communist, there were valid concerns by the Western nations that the Vietnamese people would choose communist rule.

Life had always been difficult for the Vietnamese living under French rule. A democratic, capitalistic Vietnamese government may have been their best choice, but Ho Chi Minh and his communist supporters had the advantage of building political support for a change to communism if and when there was an opportunity.

After World War II ended, Asian colonies saw the opportunity to push for independence from Western colonialism. The British saw that they could not hold on to their colonies in India and Malaysia. Britain allowed the people of those nations to form their own democracies. French leaders resisted this trend, retaining their colonies to increase trade and helping France's chances to continue as a world power. At the time, British leaders argued that it was a mistake for the French to attempt to continue in Vietnam. The French could not overcome Ho Chi Minh's compelling nationalist message to the Vietnamese people.

Unlike Britain, the United States was willing to support French control of Vietnam as a part of America's fight against communism throughout the world. If the people of Vietnam chose to elect a communist government, allied with the communist governments of China and Russia, these allied communists would harm American interests. American leaders based this conclusion upon the "Domino theory", which predicted that a new communist government in Vietnam would eventually motivate the citizens of other Southeast Asian governments to choose communism.

American support of France's recolonization in Vietnam was hypocritical to the professed American ideal that all peoples should have the freedom to choose their own destinies. A more logical stance for America was to continue to support the French in Europe, and at the same time, refuse to assist the French return to Vietnam. America could have supported Vietnamese citizens to be free to choose their own political destiny while highlighting to the Vietnamese the benefits of democratic capitalism. This tactic might convince the Vietnamese people that capitalism, not communism, was the best choice. America's leaders did not appear to understand that the foundation of the success of the political system in America was based upon the ideal of the pursuit of life, liberty, and happiness by individual citizens, freedoms rooted in self-determination.

Instead, fear of communism motivated America's leaders to believe that stopping the spread of communism justified the use of any means in Vietnam. After their return, the French financial support of local political leaders in Vietnam continued to favor the interests of the French, to the disadvantage of the Vietnamese.

American President Harry Truman supported France, along with all of America's other World War II allies, to fight against communist takeover of governments throughout the world. Truman also assisted France's domination of other former colonies, including the African nations of Algeria and Madagascar. It is easy to be critical of Truman now, in hindsight, but immediate problems of conflict with the Soviet Union and the prevention of a nuclear war were Truman's priorities.

In 1950, American leaders learned the communists of Russia and China had formed a pact which threatened American power around the world. When communist North Korea attacked capitalist South Korea, concerns about worldwide communist aggression motivated President Truman to supply American troops to fight communism in the Korean War, which lasted for 3 years until 1953, ending in a stalemate. Fighting the Korean War wounded and killed 36,000 Americans, without obtaining any benefit. Voter dissatisfaction over American troop involvement in Korea caused Democratic President Harry Truman to lose re-election for a second term. The Republicans regained control in 1954, electing President Dwight Eisenhower, who continued Truman's strategy of making the world safe for democracy.

Even though the American government supported fascist dictators in other countries, American voters believed that this support was acceptable, so long as the dictators in those nations supported capitalism, not communism. To most voters in the United States, Vietnam was a faraway country of no particular concern. The American people believed that their government was working in America's best interests. If the French retained control of Vietnam, that was one fewer country which might turn communist. Why shouldn't America help their allies which had helped to win the war against the Nazis in Europe?

France's return to Vietnam triggered conflicts: French-supported Vietnamese politicians easily maintained military superiority over the Vietnamese communists. Not having sufficient power to resist, communist Vietnamese fighters became invisible and then began committing acts of terrorism. In response, the French transported more troops and weapons to Vietnam to try to maintain peace, but the unrest was political: French-supported Vietnamese leaders engaged in torture and brutality against any Vietnamese who were not part of the French-controlled power structure. These cruel practices were counter-productive, stoking Vietnamese resistance to French rule. China's Mao Zedong began to assist the Vietnamese communists, providing weapons and training communist supporters in Vietnam to fight against French rule.

Due to a weak post-World War II economy, the French proved unable to raise sufficient funds to continue their control of Vietnam.

American diplomats, aware that France could not support the expense, insisted that the French continue to fight against the communists in Vietnam, as proxies for the capitalists. American leaders agreed to help fund the French presence in Vietnam as an attractive stop-gap measure to support capitalism. Given how much the Vietnamese people disliked French rule, it was hypocritical for America to support the French presence. It was not right for America, the land of the free, to enable France to continue its un-democratic domination of Vietnam.

American financial support in Vietnam was a "quid pro quo" for France to support American plans to rebuild Europe after World War II. American leaders were also concerned about the possibility that communists might gain control of the governments in Greece, Italy, France, and Turkey. President Truman had vowed to protect the capitalist governments of any country that might fall to communism. Ironically, these promises from America resulted in America supporting oppressive, fascist governments in Spain, Central America, South America, and South Africa, in addition to America supporting French control of Vietnam.

By 1953, American leaders increased their financial support of the French in Vietnam, agreeing to pay 80% of France's costs to remain Vietnam, amounting to $1 billion dollars per year. (In today's money, that sum would be $15 billion dollars per year.) Corporate America, particularly the manufacturers and suppliers of goods to the French, applauded increased American government spending. American manufacturers produced massive quantities of material for use by the French military in Vietnam at the expense of American taxpayers. Americans transported sophisticated, light and heavy military weapons to Vietnam, where the French military helped to maintain control and fight against communist rebels. Political donations from American corporations kept American political leaders in power who supported the concept of sending American weapons and money to support other capitalist nations around the world.

British leaders understood the futility of France's efforts based upon Britain's own experience with its colonies. Britain had already agreed to allow its former colonies, Egypt and India, to become free. No matter how hard France fought for control of Vietnam or how much support came from America, British leaders felt that France would fail. British analysts wrote news articles predicting that American support would not prevent Vietnamese communists from gaining control.

Ignoring the warnings from Britain, American leaders did not hesitate to continue the difficult and expensive quest of keeping the world safe for democracy. Ironically, America's efforts in Vietnam discouraged the Vietnamese from choosing democracy, aware that America was funding the French domination in Vietnam. The Vietnamese could see that the vast majority of military equipment used by the French was American-made. The people of Vietnam perceived that America was just another oppressing colonial power, a joint adventurer with France.

Under French rule, there had been few programs to educate peasants. Underground communist guerrilla freedom fighters called the Vietminh promised to institute educational programs for the youth of Vietnam, along with redistribution of farmland to Vietnam's peasants, once the communist government took power. At the same time, the Vietminh employed the communist tactics used in Russia and China: ruthless guerrilla fighters brutally attacked or assassinated any Vietnamese who cooperated with the French.

Most Vietnamese people sought peace, but peace was not possible. The warring forces of capitalism and communism trapped the peasants in the middle. The promise of independence under the communists was more appealing than continuing under the French, who demonstrated disrespect and a lack of concern for Vietnamese well-being. More Vietnamese came to believe that they had a chance to share in the wealth of the nation, as well as a chance for a better life, when the communists finally controlled Vietnam.

In 1953, France's recolonization of Vietnam ended, due to a military disaster at the battle of Dien Bien Phu, where 60,000 communist troops attacked an encampment of 12,000 French fighters. The communist assault at Dien Bien Phu succeeded because the French military had underestimated the number of troops that the communist leaders could muster. The French also underestimated the ability of the Vietminh fighters, who fought fiercely and were fully committed to seizing control of their own lands.

China's communist government had supplied the Vietminh with sophisticated artillery. Their troops had appeared, without warning, surrounding the French encampment. Massive artillery projectiles landed within the French encampment, while Vietminh troops devastated the French forces with heavy fire. French Mercenary troops deserted. The Vietminh troops eventually overran the French positions.

Following the defeat at Dien Bien Phu, the French and the Vietminh representatives met at a peace conference in Geneva, Switzerland. They reached an agreement known as the Geneva Accords of 1954, partitioning Vietnam into two separate nations: North Vietnam and South Vietnam. Maintaining its capital in Hanoi, the new communist government of North Vietnam would rule the people of the North. South Vietnam would remain a democracy, with its capital in Saigon.

America had refused to participate in the settlement Accords in Geneva. John Foster Dulles, leader of the American delegation to the Accords, intentionally insulted the Chinese Premier Chou En Lai by refusing to shake hands because Chou was a communist. Dulles also refused to sign the Accords, because the partition legitimized a communist government in North Vietnam. The American delegation had argued that the agreement was undesirable, as Russia and China would eventually help the Viet Minh to transform all of Vietnam into communism.

Decades later, long after the War in Vietnam ended, the discovery of communist documents from that time revealed that neither Russia nor China had wanted any entanglement with America or France in Vietnam. Russian and Chinese leaders were chiefly concerned with maintaining political control within their own countries. Neither nation could afford the amount of spending required to fight foreign wars. Both Russia and China wanted to avoid positioning themselves in direct conflict with the Americans, who had already shown a willingness to use the atomic bomb to end World War II. America might initiate a nuclear attack against Russia and China, if given an excuse to do so.

John Foster Dulles' speeches and comments in the news of the time persuaded Americans of the need to fight against communism anywhere in Southeast Asia. Without John Foster Dulles, the United States might have modified the Truman Doctrine so that America could have taken a more moderate position with regard to Vietnam.

After reaching an agreement for the Partition of Vietnam in Geneva, the French refused to make a smooth transition to assist the governments of now-bifurcated Vietnam. The Vietnamese people saw France's lack of consideration as further proof of French disregard for their welfare. The partitioning was high-stress: merchants and capitalists with homes and businesses in the North abandoned them, fleeing with their families to South Vietnam.

As part of the Partition process, communists living in the South relocated to the North. Ignoring its agreement reached in the Geneva Accords, the North Vietnamese government secretly ordered 10,000 communist fighters to remain undercover in the South, for use if and when North Vietnam ordered. The communists were physically indistinguishable from other Vietnamese. It was not long before these underground communist troops, known as the Viet Cong, created terror in South Vietnam, continuing to apply pressure for regime change, to reunify all of Vietnam with a communist government.

After the French withdrew, the American government sent advisers to Vietnam to help the South Vietnamese government continue the fight for democracy in South Vietnam. Aware that American voters were unlikely to support sending American troops to fight in Vietnam, so soon after the unpopular Korean war, the American government downplayed the role of these advisers, many of whom were secret CIA operatives, spies, and influencers sent to protect American interests.

After Partition, the government of North Vietnam took control of its citizens. Individual rights were few. North Vietnam's communist government maintained central control: Spies in every neighborhood reported anyone who was anti-patriotic or anti-communist. There was no private property remaining in North Vietnam. All homes, businesses, private property, and land had been confiscated and were completely under the control of the North Vietnamese government.

As is typical with most communist governments in the 20th century, the collectivization of land in North Vietnam proved to be a disaster. Mismanagement of farming by the new communist government resulted in famine. People faced chronic hunger and near-starvation. The economy of North Vietnam was frail. People had little control over their lives. Communist party doctrine did not allow dissent. Citizens had little access to news or information generated outside of North Vietnam. This new form of oppression came from their own communist government. Despite the failings of their communist government, most in the North felt that the situation was better than under the French. The common people hoped that life would get better as time passed.

Before the partition of Vietnam, life for the peasants in the South of Vietnam had always been much easier than life in the North, due to the fertility of the Southern land. The Mekong River Delta deposited fertile soil in the South, causing the surrounding land to be much easier to farm than the hard, rocky soil in North Vietnam. Peasants had to be tough to survive living in the North. Communism was especially attractive in the North, because of the hardships the peasants had always known, and how difficult their lives had always been. Communism promised to make things better for them.

The North Vietnamese considered the people of South Vietnam to be soft, because it was much easier to live in the South. For this same reason, communism was not as appealing to the peasants of the South. There was a better chance that a democratic government could be successful in South Vietnam. Immediately after partition, the South Vietnamese would have accepted a democratic government with a capitalistic economy, so long as that government met the needs of the South Vietnamese. But the same corrupt South Vietnamese officials, whom the French had backed, continued to control the politics of the South, now supported by American advisors behind the scenes. The South Vietnamese officials continued their corrupt self-enrichment, just as they had under the French, abusing their power in the South.

Following partition, with the assistance of backroom American support, the prime minister of South Vietnam became Ngo Dinh Diem. From the start, outside observers agreed that Diem was incompetent and lacked charisma. America supported Diem, because the American leaders did not know anyone else in South Vietnam who could be a better leader.

Diem's Catholicism was appealing to Christian American leaders, such as the Dulles brothers and other American leaders who had graduated from Yale, famous for its Christian missionary graduates, as Diem's religion was Catholic. The French had introduced Catholicism into Vietnam in the prior century. Diem showed obvious favoritism to Catholics over followers of other religions. Most Vietnamese were not Catholic. Diem tyrannically ignored the laws of Vietnam when it was convenient. His actions were arbitrary and unfair. Despite Diem's obvious inadequacies as a leader, America's CIA funding kept Diem in power.

Diem's government favored South Vietnam's upper classes, and brutally repressed the lower classes. His officials siphoned off American money to line their own pockets, and to bribe government employees, high-ranking and low, including police and hospital employees.

South Vietnamese leaders arranged lenient sentences for their supporters convicted of crimes. These same leaders elevated their military friends to desirable assignments and transferred enemies to the worst possible locations. They gave their friends business licenses, contracts with good pay and easy jobs. Political enemies accused of crimes suffered convictions based upon insufficient evidence and were often sentenced to death. If they supported the right people working in the South Vietnam government, criminals would receive light sentences.

Long before South Vietnam's first elections in 1956, held due to the Geneva Accords, intelligence information obtained by the CIA indicated that Diem and his corrupt supporters would lose to any communist candidate who ran against Diem in this 1956 election. Well aware of Diem's shortcomings, and the corrupt manner in which the current government operated, the majority of citizens of South Vietnam would vote to change, favoring the communists.

Instead of looking for other alternatives to the poor leadership Diem displayed, American advisors ignored Diem's inadequacies. The

American military and the CIA, using money and dirty tricks, helped to engineer a 98.2% election vote in favor of Diem in 1956. No honest election could ever result in so high a winning percentage.

It was obvious to political observers throughout the world that the South Vietnamese government had become a puppet of America. News broadcasts from America proclaimed that free elections had taken place in Vietnam, when in fact, the American government had fixed the presidential election to prevent a communist win. The American leaders in Vietnam did not see how propping up an unfair government in South Vietnam hindered the chances of the South Vietnamese electing democratic capitalist representatives. American leaders used their power to control South Vietnam in an unprincipled demonstration of oppressive capitalism.

The 1956 election results harmed America's credibility with the leaders of other nations who knew that this lopsided election result could only have been the product of a fixed election. It was hypocritical for American leaders to fix foreign elections while still trumpeting that America believed that all nations should have the freedom to elect their own leaders. One can argue that the American leaders' fear of communism justified interference in local politics, but there was no appreciation by the Americans that underhanded interference sent a message to the South Vietnamese and other nations that democratic governments were inferior to Communist governments. Why did America need to fix an election if its capitalist system was so superior?

Controlling elections in South Vietnam was expedient, but Diem's re-election proved that America was controlling South Vietnam through skullduggery. With the CIA's blessings, after the election, Diem continued to act in disregard of the principles of good government. If America's ultimate goal was to bring democracy to South Vietnam, there had to be a better way to do it. There was no open discussion in America about the illegal activities undertaken by the Americans in Vietnam. Most Americans were not paying close attention to events in remote Southeast Asia.

However, the American activities in Vietnam set the stage for greater problems. The situation worsened. Vietnam became a hellish place. American leaders knew that voters in the United States would never allow American involvement in Vietnam to continue, if the voters became aware of the uncontrollable chaos building in Vietnam.

If South Vietnamese voters had elected a communist government in 1956, the communist government would have confiscated all private property in South Vietnam, forcing out American business interests with the loss of all their assets in South Vietnam. There were no easy answers to the problems raised by the conflict between capitalist and communist philosophies. American financial and military power drove American decision-making, without regard to the long-term effects upon America.

The continuing infusion of cash from the CIA to the South Vietnamese government added to the corruption. The more backroom support the CIA gave to Diem, the more it fueled Diem's corrupt government at the expense of the common people of South Vietnam. At least, the Americans running Vietnam should have done their homework and helped to find and back a new, competent leader in South Vietnam who would govern all the South Vietnamese people with fairness.

Terrorism increased as the American-backed leaders in the South became increasingly disconnected from the people they were supposed to be representing. South Vietnamese leaders drove Mercedes automobiles, wore gold watches and Western clothes. In contrast, Ho Chi Minh, the communist leader of North Vietnam, dressed like a peasant. He lived in a small cottage on the grounds of the former Presidential Palace in Hanoi, the capital of North Vietnam, rejecting the opportunity to live in the lavish Palace. The message could not have been clearer: "Uncle Ho" cared about the Vietnamese people. Diem and his crew in the South were self-interested, brutal dictators, who cared only about enriching themselves and their own supporters.

Communist terrorists in South Vietnam began assassinating unpopular South Vietnamese government officials, mostly officials who had blatantly disregarded their duties to protect and assist the people in the lower economic classes. In response to the assassinations, the Diem government cruelly targeted any person identified as refusing to support Diem's regime.

In hindsight, if Diem had acted sensibly in his leadership role in the South, it is probable that democracy under Diem would have survived. Instead, his leadership was sorely lacking, and his judgment was terrible. He alienated the majority of people in the South. Communism attracted Vietnamese youth by offering to share the wealth of the country. Backed with American money and weapons, Diem was unconcerned with the dissatisfaction of the younger generation and the oppressed lower classes. The longer Diem remained in power, the more harm he did to America's reputation in South Vietnam.

In 1960, communist terrorists in South Vietnam staged coordinated attacks against South Vietnamese military forces. America responded by increasing its spending. Diem used none of the American money he received to improve life in South Vietnam. Seeing that the situation continued to deteriorate, American leaders provided more American "advisors" to assist. In 1961, the famous Green Beret American special forces arrived in South Vietnam. Additional Americans from the military, government, and private sectors in the next two years. By 1963, there were 16,000 Americans on the ground in South Vietnam. American leaders believed that they could solve the political problems of Vietnam militarily. As more Americans arrived, the communists pointed to this increased American presence as proof that America wanted to rule over South Vietnam and dominate the Vietnamese people.

Sending more Americans to South Vietnam placed more Americans in harm's way. Attempting to lessen the risk, American military leaders embraced the concept of "Air Power" as a means to wage war from a distance, making it less likely Americans would die in fighting. But fighting a war with military forces did not make sense where a defective political situation was the problem. If the communists continued to threaten South Vietnam after American-backed military successes, there was no benefit to achieving any military success in the first place.

A secret American military analysis of the situation at that time concluded that winning required 500,000 American and South Vietnamese troops to defeat the communists in South Vietnam. The analysis also indicated that no amount of bombing would defeat the government of North Vietnam.

American Presidents ignored these conclusions years later when they ordered the strategic bombing of North Vietnam, and later increased the intensity of the bombing. American leaders assured the public that the bombing was winning the war. The use of this false narrative of likely victory was effective: most American people believed that America was winning the war in Vietnam.

LESSON 27: *Opportunities to avoid a bad outcome will appear from time to time. Leaders need to recognize them and take advantage of them.*

As mediators, we often see that there are points in time where opportunities arise to negotiate. 16,000 Americans were already on the ground in South Vietnam by 1962. The leaders in America knew that further escalation of conflict was likely, but there was little discussion about how to resolve this conflict. The situation presented an opportunity to consider withdrawing from Vietnam.

The Cuban missile crisis in 1962 interrupted efforts to effectively deal with the Vietnam problem. This crisis became a much more visible problem than Vietnam. The Soviets, collaborating with Cuban leader Fidel Castro, developed the ability to initiate a "First Strike" with nuclear missiles. Due to the installation of Russian-made nuclear missiles in Cuba, close to America's mainland, these missiles could destroy American cities before American military defenses could have any opportunity to respond. The Soviet Union eventually removed these missiles from Cuba after a political stand-off with Russia where then American President John Kennedy demanded Soviet Premier Nikita Khrushchev remove the missiles, or America would attack Cuba.

Premier Khrushchev gave in to President Kennedy's demands, although American leaders made unpublicized concessions to the Soviets regarding European security issues, in return for removing the missiles. President John Kennedy recognized that Vietnam was a difficult problem, but he had kept the Vietnam situation in the background as much as possible, as there were no easy or clear answers.

The political situation in Saigon, the capital of South Vietnam, worsened on Buddha's birthday in 1963, when more than a thousand Buddhists congregated outside a radio station in Saigon to celebrate and listen to a radio broadcast by a prominent Buddhist monk. Diem's officials canceled the radio broadcast before it started, without explanation. This religious event had no potential for harm. Diem's interference was completely unfair and unnecessary. Diem's soldiers arrived in armored cars and began dispersing the crowd. Angered, the

Buddhists refused to disperse. In response, Diem's soldiers opened fire with guns, killing a woman and eight children.

Despite causing this unnecessary massacre, Diem refused to apologize for the unwarranted violence. In protest, an older Buddhist monk set himself on fire with gasoline in a Saigon public square and burned to death. Photographs of the monk sitting on the pavement with a grimace upon his face while covered in flames became front-page news around the world. Storms of protests by Buddhists within Vietnam continued. Diem's government arrested four hundred Buddhist monks and nuns. The Viet Cong responded to this unrest with increased terrorism. As a result, the police instituted curfews as a way to limit opportunities for terrorism.

Finally, American advisors in South Vietnam began pressuring Diem to change his ways. Private discussions took place among American leaders on whether to remove financial support from Diem. President Kennedy would be running for re-election, and there was concern that further deterioration of the Vietnam situation might prevent his re-election, in the same way that President Harry Truman lost re-election in 1952 for pursuing the unpopular Korean War.

Later in 1963, American President John Kennedy died, assassinated under circumstances which remain controversial. For a time, American leaders were not concerned with America's comparatively small involvement in Vietnam, the shock of the assassination of an American president in the political forefront. The American government did not consider Vietnam during the period of mourning and healing of the American nation. American leaders needed time to investigate the cause of the assassination and process the implications of the assassination. Vice-President Lyndon Johnson had become President, and his initial focus was on improving Civil Rights, not on international politics. Johnson's major interest was to improve conditions for the disadvantaged, poor and needy in America.

During 1963 and 1964, the American economy was booming. Government spending allowed American arms manufacturers to profit from building weapons and armaments for use in Vietnam. Americans were primarily concerned about social unrest within America, particularly racial segregation and discrimination.

The news media reported about events in Vietnam, but this subject was not yet at the forefront of the news. Most Americans assumed that American leaders were doing their best to look out for America's interests.

During this time, in communist North Vietnam, a typical citizen ate only four ounces of meat per day, often obtained from dogs and cats. There were protests and scattered violence arising from hardships in North Vietnam, but most North Vietnamese accepted their difficult lives. Their leaders did not allow dissent, and strictly controlled political discussion. Ho Chi Minh and Prime Minister Pham Van Dong were the faces whom the public recognized. The highly proficient shadow leader named Le Duan remained behind the scenes, as he led international policymaking for North Vietnam. Le Duan believed in self-sufficiency, that only the North Vietnamese could create their own freedom. His experience was that past financial and military support from Russia and China had been unreliable.

Le Duan arranged for increased terrorism to disrupt South Vietnam, rather than initiating armed combat by sending North Vietnamese troops into South Vietnam. Le Duan feared that open aggression by North Vietnam could draw in more American military support to fight against his people. Le Duan insisted that outsiders see the source of terrorism in the South as an independent revolutionary movement from within South Vietnam. He did not want to reveal that this terrorism originated in North Vietnam, even though communist leaders in the North directed the Viet Cong fighters in the South.

The Viet Cong started assassinating provincial officials in villages of South Vietnam, one by one, which motivated other South Vietnamese officials to quickly relocate to Saigon, the capital, or to other cities within South Vietnam, to obtain personal security not available in the countryside.

The Viet Cong brutally butchered local provincial officials and their families who remained in rural areas, which caused other officials to withdraw to large cities for their own protection. Their departure allowed the Viet Cong to take control of rural villages, distributing the land of the murdered or missing officials to the local peasants, buying their loyalty. At the same time, the confiscation of the land of the assassinated officials sent the message to peasants in nearby areas that alignment with the communist rebels was less dangerous and could be rewarding, as the peasants who supported the Viet Cong received land. This was only one of the ways that the communists garnered popular support to overthrow South Vietnam's corrupt government.

Increased Viet Cong terrorism triggered violent retribution by the government of South Vietnam. In response to Diem's crackdown, Viet Cong terrorists used children to toss hand grenades into cafes and markets, further destabilizing Saigon. Concerned about Diem's ability to govern, American officials searched for a replacement leader for South Vietnam. Rumors of American dissatisfaction with Diem added to the unstable situation. Even though it was rumored that Diem would fly out of South Vietnam to a safe country, his own officers assassinated Diem, providing the opportunity for American advisers to choose a new leader for South Vietnam.

American leaders must have tacitly agreed to Diem's assassination, as the South Vietnamese military would never have taken steps against Diem unless given reassurances that America would not create an issue if Diem died. The lesson learned by the people of South Vietnam was that they could not trust the Americans. Why support a corrupt democracy that failed to provide security to cooperating Vietnamese?

Back in America, most people believed that South Vietnamese fighters against communism deserved American support. American news reporters noticed that the news releases from American government sources contradicted news stories written by journalists in Saigon. Nor did news reports in America jive with the disturbing accounts returning soldiers gave about their experiences in Vietnam: There was no straightforward way to distinguish the "good guys" from the "bad guys." Soldiers returning to America did not report progress to win the war, nor did it appear likely to see progress in the future. At this time, America could have walked away from South Vietnam. What was the purpose of America continuing to stay in South Vietnam?

North Vietnam increased its terrorist pressure in South Vietnam. Le Duan also began organizing attacks by communist troops from North Vietnam. He had come to believe that successful attacks by North Vietnamese armies would discourage America, resulting in Vietnam eventually becoming reunified. But when North Vietnamese armies advanced into South Vietnam, American leaders committed more troops to fight in South Vietnam, fearing that a failure to respond to the North Vietnamese attacks would risk damaging America's reputation as a dependable ally and world leader. Unfortunately, to obtain political support for bringing more American troops to Vietnam, American leaders falsely told American voters that there was progress toward victory over the communists.

LESSON 28: *Nations should implement procedures for continuing assessment and re-evaluation of any existing conflict, identifying bad decisions and rectifying the situation when possible.*

If American leaders had disclosed the true state of affairs in South Vietnam, American voters would not have approved sending additional troops. By hiding the truth, American leaders betrayed their own citizens, and, at the same time, betrayed the people of South Vietnam. No one can justify the concept of sending American soldiers and civilians to Vietnam under false pretenses of probable victory. For their own political gains, American politicians sacrificed the American ideals of fairness, freedom, and self-determination. These unprincipled leaders were likely to lose re-election upon disclosure of their actions. It was poor judgment to continue the conflict, being aware that the war was futile, wasteful, and homicidal to large numbers of people.

If American leaders had valued innocent lives over their own political ambitions, more stability would have come to Southeast Asia. To end the Vietnam War at that time would have required American leaders to admit their mistakes. President Lyndon Johnson later confessed his worry that voters would brand him a coward if America stopped supporting the government of South Vietnam. If the Americans returned home without having gained anything in return for losses of lives and enormous expenditures of tax money, they would blame him. Johnson was worried that opposition Republicans would paint him an "appeaser," harkening back to the time of World War II when Britain's appeasement of Hitler had aided the Nazis' successful aggression in Europe.

Ironically, President Johnson's decision to escalate the Vietnam War did more harm to his political future than if he simply had told the American people that the purpose of the Vietnam War had ended and that the Vietnamese would have to work things out on their own. Johnson was short-sighted, even assuming that he was being honest about his decision-making priorities. Uninterrupted American support enabled corrupt South Vietnamese leaders to play their own political games, pursuing wealth and power, continuing to ignore the welfare of the people of South Vietnam.

President Johnson said that he was not going to go down into history as the President who lost Vietnam. Yet, we now know that his advisors had warned Johnson at the beginning of his presidency that the Vietnam War was not winnable. Johnson "passed the buck" to the next president. His decisions caused the loss of more American lives and also caused massive numbers of deaths and injuries of Vietnamese people, in both North and South Vietnam.

It is difficult to settle disputes when one side of the controversy is not willing to listen to reason. Here, President Johnson's decisions were based on politics, made without regard to the consequences for the people involved. He did not see, or his subordinates were not forceful enough to convince him to see, that he could have "sold" the American people that America needed to withdraw from Vietnam. By this time, the majority of American newspaper reporters and editors were writing that the Vietnam War was not proceeding as expected. The media would have supported bringing the American troops home, had President Johnson chosen to end America's involvement in Vietnam during his presidency.

President Johnson did not recognize that he was in a lose–lose situation. He had a reputation for being a hard-headed bully. Were his own top people afraid to tell him the truth? Were the people further down the political pecking order afraid to tell their superiors the truth?

LESSON 29: *Leaders must value truth to ensure that the best information can find its way to the top. People have to say what they think, and be prepared to look for new employment, if they find they are working for leaders who encourage lies and deception. To do otherwise is to be complicit in wrongdoing.*

As a consequence of the failure of America to withdraw from South Vietnam, Saigon continued its transformation into a dirty, crowded wartime metropolis, teeming with American soldiers spending American money chasing alcohol, drugs, and women. Terrorism by Viet Cong guerrillas increased. American airpower bombarded the peasantry of South Vietnam, killing and wounding untold numbers. American officials in Vietnam were complicit in supporting the Vietnamese underground economy, as were American corporations doing business in South Vietnam. Saigon was filled with bars and brothels, where illegal activities took place, funded in part by the salaries of American soldiers and civilians.

A number of American officials and corporations were heavily involved in money laundering and bribery in South Vietnam. The communist Viet Cong used American corruption to convince young South Vietnamese men that only communism could help return South Vietnam to a degree of honesty and fairness, to improve the way that the common people lived, to a way of life where their women could be free from prostitution, and the men could farm in peace or participate in respectable businesses.

American military leaders and politicians could not agree: Should they use overwhelming force, and if so, against whom? The Viet Cong in the South or the North Vietnamese in North Vietnam? Or should America withdraw? American leaders were concerned about American humiliation. They were also concerned that escalation in Vietnam might draw China into a global war.

President Johnson appointed General William Westmoreland as the new leader of American military forces in Vietnam. General Westmoreland told President Johnson that America was winning and would be victorious. He disregarded the reality of the situation and chose to tell President Johnson what Johnson wanted to hear.

The South Vietnamese military claimed that they were carrying their load of fighting, but the reality was that American troops were doing the heavy fighting. This situation is reminiscent of the American colonial militias' participation in the war with the French before the American Revolution. The British had a stronger interest in fighting, and the colonials took the wise course of sitting back whenever possible, letting the British forces manage the dirty work. In this same way, the South Vietnamese military kept in the background and let the Americans do the fighting, to the extent possible.

As the 1964 American Presidential election neared, American military forces staged secret raids into North Vietnam. The Americans also sent a warship to the coast of North Vietnam, to allow American special forces to stage additional secret raids. When North Vietnamese navy vessels entered their own coastal waters to investigate the presence of the American warship, the Americans opened fire on the North Vietnamese vessels without warning.

The official American statement to the press about this incident deceptively claimed that the North Vietnamese had initiated the attack. Despite the fact that the Americans were the ones who started firing first, the American government dispatched a stern warning to the North Vietnamese leaders that any further "unprovoked" attacks on American warships by the North Vietnamese would have grave consequences. The Americans did not mention that it was the entry of the American warship into the coastal waters of North Vietnam which had provoked the incident.

The American warship remained in the waters near the coast of North Vietnam. American leaders claimed that the North Vietnamese had made a further attack upon the American warship, although there was no reliable proof of any attack. To the contrary, later investigation revealed that the North Vietnamese navy had approached solely to rescue their damaged boats from the first incident. Their sailors had explicit orders not to attack the American warship.

Based on the false claims by the American military that the North Vietnamese initiated attacks on the American warship, President Johnson announced to the press that America made a retaliatory air strike against North Vietnamese airbases. Johnson's statement was a lie, made to justify air strikes on North Vietnam. American voters would not tolerate the obvious unfairness of this incident, had the truth been known. It is likely that the Johnson Administration ordered the air raids against North Vietnam to make President Johnson look more powerful in the lead-up to the 1964 election.

President Johnson won reelection in 1964 by a landslide, through successfully (and ironically) portraying his conservative republican opponent Barry Goldwater as being likely to send American soldiers to their deaths in unnecessary wars, which is exactly what Johnson himself had undertaken with his unjustified air attacks on the people of North Vietnam, in the process risking many American lives and wasting American taxpayer money to underwrite the cost of the 1964 air bombing.

These unjustified American bombing raids unified the North Vietnamese people against America. North Vietnamese leaders had no choice but to respond aggressively to unprovoked bombings. Before these unjustified attacks, fear of American aggression had restrained North Vietnamese aggression. What was the point of North Vietnam holding back if the Americans were going to attack regardless of what North Vietnam did?

Following the onset of the American bombing in North Vietnam, China dramatically increased its donations of advanced weaponry to the North Vietnamese, including MIG jet fighters and Chinese military advisors. Chinese leaders were careful to avoid direct provocation of America. They had an agreement with Le Duan that North Vietnamese troops would undertake all fighting, using Chinese-supplied weapons. At the same time, Le Duan requested the underground communist Viet Cong intensify terror attacks within South Vietnam.

Documents from that era revealed that the Soviet Union had urged the leaders of North Vietnam *not* to escalate the war. The Soviets had also provided the North Vietnamese with weapons, but neither China nor the Soviets would agree to provide their troops. Neither Russia nor China wanted to risk provoking conflict directly with America.

President Johnson was re-elected, in part because he promised that he would not send American troops to fight a war that the Asian troops should be fighting. Knowing that America had little chance to win this war, once he was re-elected, President Johnson could have arranged for a gradual withdrawal from South Vietnam. Instead, Johnson announced that America would continue to assist the people of South Vietnam. The American people reacted positively. They believed the press releases from American officials, which projected confidence in American victory over the communists. Little knowledge of the reality on the ground filtered through to the American people. American casualties in Vietnam were still comparatively limited.

American leaders in Vietnam continued to manage the South Vietnamese leaders. Yet the American leaders could not hide the truth forever. Information regarding American secrets leaked to local newspapers from South Vietnamese military officers. By 1965, the Viet Cong had grown more powerful. President Johnson's advisors provided him with intelligence reports concluding that it was highly unlikely that America could win the war. In the South Vietnamese capital of Saigon, life became more difficult. Most young people in rural areas either became Viet Cong guerrillas, or moved to the major cities for protection from Viet Cong fighters.

As more American soldiers arrived, the fighting escalated. American troops on the ground were frequently attacked by the Viet

Cong. In response to these casualties, the American government countered by ordering massive bombing attacks on North Vietnam. American leaders avoided ground fighting against the Viet Cong, to save the lives of American soldiers.

Despite the ill will President Johnson had engendered with the North Vietnamese, Johnson believed that America could buy its way out of the conflict. He decided to offer the North Vietnamese $1 billion to help build a Mekong River Dam if the North Vietnamese would agree to stop the fighting. President Johnson was surprised when the North Vietnamese ignored his offer. He failed to understand the fervor of the North Vietnamese to free their country from foreign control. Why should they trust Americans who had made up false stories to justify unprovoked American attacks? When the North Vietnamese did not respond to his offer, President Johnson further escalated the American bombing of North Vietnam. If Johnson had better advice or Johnson had listened to good advice that came his way, Johnson might have made the better choice to withdraw American forces from this unwinnable war, as soon as possible.

American bombing of North Vietnam increased in the years that followed: By the end of the bombing, United States B-52 Bombers had dropped a total of four million tons (4,000,000 x 2000 pounds) of bombs in North Vietnam and South Vietnam. There was no proportion between the enormous number of bombs dropped by America and any benefit the bombing could bring. The tremendous expense of fighting the Vietnam War caused high inflation, devaluing the American dollar, and later causing a deep economic recession in America, starting in the mid-1970s, lasting until 1984. Fighting the Vietnam War did not do any good. Instead, major financial problems appeared. Inflation hurt the spending power of all Americans because their government wasted taxpayer money to fight this lost cause.

By the end of 1965, the American government maintained more than 175,000 American troops in Vietnam. The government made this major commitment to American troops without identifying any reasonable objective that these troops could accomplish. US Army General Bruce Palmer later wrote that "American troops were fighting a formless war against a formless enemy," impossible to control. Injuries and deaths of American soldiers were increasing. If the truth – that this was a hopeless situation – had become public at this time, the fighting could have stopped. Other American leaders had tried to publicize the truth about Vietnam, but it was hard to fight against the propaganda that any American who spoke out against the war in Vietnam was being unpatriotic.

By 1966, even American Defense Secretary Robert McNamara privately acknowledged that the Vietnam War was no longer winnable. He had the option of resigning as Secretary of Defense. This action would have brought public attention to McNamara's honest opinion that the conflict in Vietnam was unwinnable. McNamara's resignation would have created political pressure on President Johnson to reconsider his strategy. Instead, Robert McNamara remained as Johnson's Defense Secretary for almost two more years. McNamara participated in the massive intensifying of fighting in Vietnam, even though he knew there was little hope of obtaining any benefit. Defense Secretary McNamara eventually moved to the background in the news, letting Dean Rusk, then the Secretary of State, become President Johnson's main spokesperson in favor of continuing to fight the war in Vietnam.

The South Vietnamese had not learned how American politics worked. They did not know that the free press in America was available to them if they wanted to expose the reality of American involvement and the lack of progress in fighting against the communists. The Vietnamese believed that the President and other wealthy and powerful Americans controlled America. They had no idea that the American people possessed the power to make changes to the American leadership. Only later, when massive protests against the war took place in America, did the American people show the world their power to effect changes in leadership.

Conditions in Saigon deteriorated further: Eight more Buddhist monks and nuns burned themselves to death to protest the government's arrest of opposition political supporters. The Saigon police dragged monks and nuns out from the sanctuary of Buddhist temples. The Viet Cong declared June 1966 "Hate America Month."

At the same time, the American military increased bombing, striking multiple locations in South Vietnam, as well as in North Vietnam, killing large numbers of civilians. The Viet Cong continued brutal assassinations and executions in South Vietnam.

The American military announced the "discovery" that the Viet Cong were part of a world-wide communist conspiracy seeking to take over all of Southeast Asia. American officials reassured the American public that American bombing raids in South Vietnam had no negative effect on South Vietnamese civilians. Multiple sources outside the American government disagreed. They reported that America was hurting, not helping the people of South Vietnam.

General Westmoreland then stated that he needed 700,000 more American troops deployed in order to win in South Vietnam. The Joint Chiefs of Staff at the Pentagon refused General Westmoreland's request, stating that 500,000 more American troops were sufficient to win in Vietnam.

President Johnson had a choice: If he withdrew American forces from Vietnam on the basis that the war was one for the South Vietnamese military to fight, that American interest in Vietnam was limited, and because the risk to American lives did not justify proceeding, Johnson might have been re-elected President two years later in 1968. But President Johnson did not take this opportunity to extricate America from this war.

By the end of 1966, 385,000 American military and civilian personnel occupied South Vietnam, with more in transit. The cost to America that year for fighting the war was over $15 Billion. In the following year, the cost of America's involvement had grown to $17 Billion. To help fund the war, President Johnson requested a surcharge to increase the individual federal income and corporate taxes on Americans by 6% for 1967.

Accurate news about the conflict in Vietnam eventually found its way to the American public. However, most Americans still trusted that their government leaders were telling the truth, that America was doing the right thing by continuing to fight in Vietnam.

American bombing crews had no way to tell whether they were bombing communist fighters or not. In addition to explosive bombs, American airplanes dropped a flaming petroleum jelly, called "Napalm," on civilians and homes in those villages suspected of supporting the communists.

North Vietnamese leaders publicized their large numbers of civilian casualties due to American bombing, which created bad optics for the American government. North Vietnam's military placed missile launchers and weapons close to civilian centers and soccer stadiums in the capital city of Hanoi, believing that the Americans would not risk bombing those areas for fear of striking civilians. American leaders modified their bombing methods, attempting to avoid the bad press from civilian casualties. The high command ordered American pilots to avoid bombing within ten miles of Hanoi, which made the bombing less effective. Americans stopped bombing harbors for fear of striking Soviet ships, to lower the risk of drawing the Soviet Union into a war with America.

Improved North Vietnamese weapons were able to shoot down more American aircraft. The loss of more aircraft forced a change in strategy: the Americans then bombed from higher altitudes to lower their risk from anti-aircraft fire. Bombing from a higher altitude impaired accuracy. Errant bombings killed and wounded North Vietnamese civilians, creating more bad press for America.

There was no lasting benefit from the American bombing. Terrorizing people on the ground did not discourage them. Rather, the extensive bombing strengthened the communists' will to fight. The North Vietnamese civilians adapted their daily lives to minimize harm. Military leaders of North Vietnam reorganized their operations to minimize the effect of the bombings. Trains were set up to run on coal rather than oil. This made the bombing of North Vietnamese oil facilities less able to interfere with the North's ability to transport troops and supplies. To avoid attack, communist troops usually moved at night, under cover of the extensive vegetation.

As early as the spring of 1967, American political protests against the Vietnam War expanded. Entertainers and other celebrities joined the protesters to stop the war. Bitter Vietnam veterans related horrific experiences, highlighting the ineffectiveness of American efforts to combat the communists.

Not surprisingly, the next wave of American soldiers sent to Vietnam contained a sizable percentage who were less motivated to fight, used drugs and complained about their circumstances. Anti-war protesters called the American troops wanton killers, bringing an unjust and useless war. These protests upset patriotic American troops who were fighting in South Vietnam. Draft avoidance became more popular. Where families could afford the cost, young men decided to go to college, which at that time exempted them from military service, to avoid Vietnam. Voluntarily joining the American National Guard also assured young men that their military service would not station them in Vietnam. Poor or uneducated draftees could not avoid fighting in Vietnam.

In contrast, North Vietnamese leader Ho Chi Minh's inspirational speeches convinced his communist supporters that it was necessary to fight in this war to obtain their freedom from foreign rule. American bombing attacks on North Vietnam increased the popularity of the North Vietnamese government. North Vietnamese people were eager to fight back, their resolve hardened by the bombing. It was easy to rally young North Vietnamese men to fight for freedom and independence. They hated the Americans for bringing this war.

The Soviet and Chinese governments provided more missile launchers and technicians to help the North Vietnamese fighters deploy and repair this complex equipment. Chinese and Russian technical specialists were also able to examine downed American aircraft and other weaponry that remained after a battle, learning American technical secrets.

The American troops were not fighting a traditional war. Instead of attempting to gain control of the ground, the destruction of communist fighters became the goal of this war. American troops would arrive, forcing communist Viet Cong troops to leave an area. After fighting, the American troops would also leave the area, only to return a month later to find the Viet Cong had returned to the same ground. The Americans returned and again fought against Viet Cong troops in the same location, but nothing was gained. This American plan to win the war by eliminating enemy soldiers did not work. This was their homeland. Where did the Americans expect the Vietnamese people would go?

Moreover, the Viet Cong soldiers were indistinguishable from the friendly South Vietnamese. American troops did not know who might start firing a machine gun or throw a bomb. This did not help the morale of American troops. The safest approach was for American soldiers to treat any unknown person as a potential enemy. Over time, most American troops treated all of the Vietnamese suspiciously, knowing that there was no way to know who might harm them. Bad experiences with American soldiers helped recruit more young Vietnamese to become freedom fighters for the communists.

The American military claimed victories in battles, based upon enemy body counts. The number of enemy soldiers killed or wounded was considered to be an accurate marker of American success. If American troops killed or wounded enough communists, American leaders believed that these losses would discourage the communists from fighting. Relying upon body counts as a measure of victory backfired. If anything, the longer the war continued, the more Vietnamese volunteered to fight with the communists.

Counting each enemy casualty as a point on the scale of success also encouraged American soldiers to exaggerate the injuries and deaths of enemy soldiers. American troops on the ground quickly learned that their commanders wanted to see reports of high enemy body counts. Soldiers exaggerated the numbers of enemy casualties, not caring if the information was accurate, so long as it satisfied their commanding officers. Political leaders in America had an interest in trumpeting the "proof" that America was succeeding.

They told the American media that the war was progressing well. News reporters from the rest of the world were skeptical about American claims of high numbers of enemy casualties. Foreign reporters in Vietnam did not see any improvement in the American position. President Johnson's Administration intentionally ignored or hid information that could hurt Johnson politically. This obfuscation prevented accurate reappraisals of strategy by other American leaders, who might act to end the Vietnam War as soon as possible. If American voters had learned that they were being deceived by the Johnson Administration's claim that America was winning the war, the

Vietnam War could have ended quickly, with less loss of life on all sides.

In opposition to the Vietnam War, Democratic Senator Robert Kennedy, the younger brother of the assassinated Democratic President John Kennedy, declared publicly that he believed that America could not win the Vietnam War. About the same time, the government of North Vietnam proclaimed that the North Vietnamese would continue to fight as long as the Americans wanted to fight, for 20 years or more.

American soldiers were frustrated by the disconnect between what they were seeing on the ground and what American officials claimed was happening. Soldiers were glad to tell reporters the truth, that they were in a futile fight, where their best goal was to be able to survive a year of duty in Vietnam, and then transfer somewhere else. The troops could see no progress, despite large numbers of American troops fighting, and the increased amount of heavy equipment used by American military forces in the air and on the ground.

American soldiers on the ground in Vietnam were far away from home, walking in the jungle, hunting elusive enemies. It was hot, damp, and dangerous. There were mines and booby traps. The first notice of a communist attack was when the Viet Cong started shooting. The communists were on home turf and could move easily, as they carried minimal equipment. The Americans transported heavy equipment and moved slowly. At night, most Americans returned to the safety of their camps. At the same time, communist troops moved under cover of darkness.

Forced to fight with unreliable American-made automatic M-14 rifles, American soldiers in the middle of firefights with communist forces were dying unnecessarily. M-14 jamming impaired morale. The communists wielded reliable Russian AK-47 machine guns to overcome American troops. The war had momentum, which was hard to stop. Soldiers focused on fighting and survival.

Unlike the American military, the leaders in North Vietnam did not have a public relations problem. They could easily censor and control negative information. Communist soldiers, living on minimal food in hot, damp jungle conditions, heard only good news and encouragement from their leaders. Communist soldiers did suffer from weakened immune systems due to poor diets and stress. Bombs dropped from American B-52 jets were so powerful and intense that surviving North Vietnamese soldiers reported that their lives changed from the near-death experiences of being so close to the explosions of the incredibly powerful bombs, each of which left a huge crater, cut deep into the ground. Their desperate struggles to survive hardened the communist troops and made them better soldiers. The South Vietnamese soldiers were more interested in survival than in fighting.

An American presidential election was to take place in November 1968. North Vietnamese leader Le Duan hoped that a successful communist offensive in Vietnam made before this election would motivate the American government to remove its troops from Vietnam. In early 1968, under Le Duan's guidance, the North Vietnamese planned to undertake a major military offensive during the Vietnamese holiday called Tet.

The most important religious holiday in Vietnam, Tet, celebrates the arrival of spring. South Vietnamese soldiers returned home for the Tet holiday after the leaders of North and South Vietnam agreed to a truce to stop fighting for the holiday. "Intelligence" received in America indicated that North Vietnam might be ready to negotiate a solution to the war. The South Vietnamese military readily agreed to the truce. But the communist offer of a truce was just a ruse:

At the beginning of the Tet holiday, North Vietnamese communist troops, together with Viet Cong fighters in South Vietnam, jointly attacked the majority of the capital cities of the provinces throughout South Vietnam. Local district capitals were also attacked. 67,000 North Vietnamese and Viet Cong fighters, using modern military weaponry and equipment donated by the Chinese and Russian leaders, made 100 separate coordinated attacks.

The well-organized, large-scale communist Tet offensive ranged all over South Vietnam, including in its capital Saigon, the place where the American presence was greatest. Viet Cong troops boldly attacked the American Embassy in Saigon. The television news in America showed dramatic film clips of the fighting in Saigon, which shocked the American public. Dominating the international news, the communist offensive was powerful. How could America be winning the war if the communists were able to attack American troops on such a large scale, including attacking the American Embassy?

When the Tet Offensive was over, 4,000 more Americans had died, along with 6,000 South Vietnamese soldiers. Destruction of civilian dwellings created 500,000 refugees in South Vietnam. Responding to the attacks, the American military immediately requested 200,000 additional American soldiers to fight in Vietnam. The American public did not receive this request favorably. Even though communist fighters failed to obtain military success, American leaders could no longer support their false narrative that America was winning the war.

After Tet, the American news media was critical of the continuation of the Vietnam War. Fighting this war made no sense. North Vietnamese communists resolved to continue fighting indefinitely. New American Secretary of Defense Clark Clifford ordered that there would be no more forecasts of imminent victory by America. Political support for sending more American troops to Vietnam disappeared. Less than two months after the start of the Tet Offensive, the American bombing of North Vietnam halted, due to its unpopularity with American voters.

President Johnson announced that America would agree to open negotiations. Johnson then surprised everyone by abruptly stating that he would not seek re-election. This announcement left the resolution of the Vietnam problem to the next American president. Johnson had been responsible for losses of more than one million Vietnamese lives, more than 50,000 American lives, and countless injuries. As the truth came out regarding the grim reality of the situation in Vietnam, political backlash left President Johnson with a tarnished reputation despite his important achievements driving the passage of American Civil Rights laws.

It is ironic that the Tet Offensive was not a military victory. Yet, the large-scale communist attack ended America's will to fight. North Vietnamese leaders, seeing that America had lost its stomach for fighting, refused to agree to any concessions to obtain peace. Le Duan firmly and patiently waited for the opportunity to unify all of Vietnam under a communist government.

American leaders wanted to avoid the appearance of defeat. It would be embarrassing for America to withdraw without gain from this lengthy and expensive conflict. The goal of American soldiers who remained in Vietnam, aware that victory was impossible, was to survive their military service. Morale of American troops dropped even lower. Meanwhile, the North Vietnamese leadership applied additional military pressure both in North and South Vietnam, increasing American casualties. The inability to identify whether a particular Vietnamese person was friendly or unfriendly continued. Racial differences made the Americans easy targets for communist shooters.

Meanwhile, American Democratic presidential candidate Hubert Humphrey vowed to end the Vietnam War. If Humphrey won the presidential election, America would withdraw from Vietnam quickly, without seeking concessions. It is important to note, however, that neither Democratic presidential candidate Eugene McCarthy nor

Democratic presidential candidate Robert Kennedy were willing to admit American defeat, because most American voters could not accept the idea of defeat. American politicians had fed their voters propaganda that America would win in Vietnam. The voters would not easily accept that America had wasted so much money and so many lives, with no return. The Democrats had been in power since 1960 and risked defeat in the 1968 presidential election.

When a madman assassinated Democratic candidate Robert Kennedy in June of 1968, the American public went into shock. An assassin had killed President John Kennedy less than 5 years before his brother Robert met the same fate. Only 2 months before Robert Kennedy's death, a racist white man killed Martin Luther King, the best-known Black leader in America. What was the world coming to? The American public was looking for answers, looking for change, and looking for a return to stability.

American leaders were rightfully concerned about American strength. Communists and other anti-American governments in the world might try to take advantage of American instability and act against American interests. American voters chose Republican candidate Richard Nixon to become the next American president in November of 1968. A majority of Americans believed that the sooner American troops withdrew from Vietnam, the better. But American politicians were concerned about the perception of other governments. How would defeat affect American relations around the world?

LESSON 30: *Failing to seize opportunities to settle often makes resolution much more difficult later on.*

Vietnam, after the Tet Offensive, demonstrates how wars can continue to go badly in ways unforeseen at the beginning of fighting. The time for the American troops to withdraw was before the escalation of the Vietnam War, or at least, withdrawal should have taken place as soon as it was clear that the escalation of the Vietnam War was not succeeding. After years of false pronouncements of success, American leaders could not embrace a change in course.

Entering office in January 1969, President Richard Nixon did not quickly end the American involvement in South Vietnam. In November of 1969, a massacre at My Lai demonstrated what can happen when leaders deploy troops without the troops having any clear purpose. The American soldiers who engaged in the massacre at My Lai had completely lost their morality. They acted in a sort of "group psychosis," killing hundreds of Vietnamese civilian men, women, and children in the village of My Lai for no apparent reason. This civilian massacre would have been worse, but American helicopter troops rushed to the scene of the massacre when radioed about the mayhem. They stopped further executions of South Vietnamese civilians.

The senseless incident at My Lai confirmed the waste created by the presence of American troops where they did not belong. It was easy enough for American leaders to claim that this event was an aberration caused by one disturbed officer. The reality is that this sort of event would not have taken place if America had taken earlier action to withdraw. There was no valid reason for American troops to remain in Vietnam. American leaders wrongfully believed that America had an interest in remaining, to appear strong and project power. In fact, America was trampling the rights of other people to be free from unwanted domination and subjugation, abrogating the principles established in the American Constitution. American troops no longer belonged in Vietnam. As long as wars continue, all sorts of terrible things will happen that no one wants to happen, which is why it is so important to avoid war and end it as soon as possible.

President Nixon slowly withdrew troops from Vietnam, but he continued bombing and fighting, wasting more lives and money. He secretly approved sending American forces covertly into the nearby nations of Cambodia and Laos, to apply pressure on communist forces which had positioned themselves near the Vietnam border. The communists had expected safety from being in a different nation that was not engaged in war. American violations of the national borders of Laos and Cambodia caused great losses of life there. Illegal violation of other nations' borders did not help America's reputation, even if communist fighters from Vietnam were hiding there.

The Vietnam War continued into 1971. Having been in office for three years, President Nixon wanted to look strong for the upcoming Presidential election of 1972. There were hundreds of American prisoners of war (POWs) remaining in communist custody in North Vietnam. Media attention centered upon ending the war and freeing the POWs.

American troops still fighting on the ground in Vietnam had poor morale. They knew the Vietnam War would be ending, with no chance to accomplish anything positive. What soldier would want to keep fighting, knowing that risking injury or death would make no difference in the outcome for America? The exception was for career military officers looking to boost their credentials. A small number of American military units refused to fight. American officers who forced their troops to fight risked injury or death at the hands of their own troops.

Communist fighters in Vietnam attacked American troops where they had become lax in their defenses. North Vietnamese troops knew that the war would end with their victory. They had a psychological advantage over the discouraged American troops.

Not being able to obtain settlement concessions from the North Vietnamese, President Nixon ordered additional air bombing attacks against North Vietnamese installations, breaking the rules of engagement previously established by the American Military's Joint Chiefs of Staff. President Nixon resumed these air attacks to make America appear more powerful, to enhance his chances for re-election in 1972. He wanted to obtain a deal where the Vietnam war would end with agreement from all sides, allowing America to withdraw with dignity, even though Nixon knew it was inevitable that the communists would soon gain control of all of Vietnam.

Nixon was concerned about his reputation with American voters. Continuing the air attacks on North Vietnam supported the fiction that America was not losing in Vietnam, and that America would not surrender to the North Vietnamese. President Nixon felt there was a value to the bombing, to try to force the North Vietnamese to make a deal that would help him politically, despite the inevitability of American defeat and the knowledge that bombing would waste resources and lives on both sides.

At best, Nixon's continued aggression might result in allowing capitalism to survive in South Vietnam for a brief time after American troops eventually withdrew. Communist fighters could easily defeat the government of the South and reunite all of Vietnam once the Americans departed. The American public cared most about achieving the return of the remaining American troops and the American prisoners of war.

In 1971, Le Duan launched a further offensive into the South, to hasten the end of the war, despite awareness that this offensive would waste thousands of lives of his communist troops and despite his knowledge that America would exit Vietnam in the near future in any event. In part, North Vietnam launched this offensive because President Nixon had met with Chinese leaders, shrewdly inviting China to develop political and commercial relationships with America going forward. Once America and China made a deal, the Chinese military would no longer assist North Vietnam. Le Duan saw the development of an American relationship with China as a betrayal by the Chinese communists. In light of this, Le Duan acted to quickly force the reunification of Vietnam.

In March of 1972, the North Vietnamese began another large military offensive against the South. Neither China nor Russia approved, as both wanted to better their relations with America. The fighting in this final North Vietnamese offensive was the most brutal and bloody of the Vietnam War. Extensive American air power defended against the communist forces.

Eventually, the Americans made a deal with North Vietnam, and both sides were able to save face, allowing the current South Vietnamese President Thieu to remain in office. The deal with North Vietnam included provisions supporting the South Vietnamese government. Both sides knew that this agreement was a charade. Once the Americans and their military departed, South Vietnamese President Thieu's democratic government would fall.

The purpose of the American agreement with North Vietnam was cosmetic: to create optics that presented the American government in the best possible light, the main goal of which was to quell the wrath of American voters.

Recognizing that Nixon's deal with the North Vietnamese would not benefit him, South Vietnamese President Thieu refused to ratify the agreement. In turn, the North Vietnamese leaders refused to release the American POWs without Thieu's approval of the deal. President Nixon's response to this impasse was a further resumption of the bombing of North Vietnam as punishment for refusal to move forward with the deal. The war had to end soon, but once again,

President Nixon sought to teach the North Vietnamese a lesson in what later became known as "Nixon's Christmas bombing."

The resumption of the bombing of North Vietnam was expensive. American pilots and their crews risked their lives, yet there was no military goal for the bombing. North Vietnamese defenses destroyed fifteen American B-52 aircraft in these last air raids on North Vietnam. The surviving American pilots were furious about their friends on the downed B-52s losing their lives or becoming prisoners when everyone knew that the attacks would not change the outcome of the war. The North Vietnamese used film footage of these last bombings as further propaganda against America, showing photos and films of North Vietnamese civilian men, women, and children, dead and injured, as well as a hospital destroyed by the recent American bombing. Newspapers across the world reported that the Americans had acted atrociously. Commentators claimed this bombing of civilians constituted war crimes. President Nixon justified the bombing as helping to force North Vietnamese leaders to return to the negotiating table.

At the same time, President Nixon promised South Vietnamese President Nguyen Van Thieu that if communist aggression continued after the Americans left South Vietnam, American air power and ground fighting would resume to protect Thieu's government. Nixon soon after resigned for reasons unrelated to Vietnam, avoiding impeachment arising from the Watergate scandal in America, where the proof showed that Nixon lied to government investigators about his knowledge of his political operatives' illegal activities.

Incoming American President Gerald Ford reassured South Vietnamese President Thieu that America would honor Nixon's promises. But American congressional leaders, responding to the complaints from American voters, reduced funding to South Vietnam, which the South Vietnamese government needed to be able to defend itself. One reason behind Congress' funding cut was the economic recession in America and high inflation caused in part by the excessive American spending on the Vietnam War. American congressional leaders used their power over government funding to restrain any further military assaults in Vietnam and Southeast Asia by refusing to fund them.

The South Vietnamese government responded by printing money without the resources to back their currency, causing runaway inflation in South Vietnam. American money became highly valuable to the extent that the cost of a high-class prostitute in Saigon fell to only $1. With South Vietnam's economy in shambles, communist forces resumed their attacks. American government employees remaining in South Vietnam were forced to depart from Saigon in helicopters and airplanes on an emergency basis.

America abandoned Thieu and the South Vietnamese government. In their rush to escape, the Americans never destroyed records listing the South Vietnamese citizens who had assisted or worked to help the Americans. The failure of the departing Americans to destroy these records allowed incoming communist forces to learn the identity of South Vietnamese citizens who had cooperated with Americans. The communists began mass executions of South Vietnamese who had not already found a way to escape. South Vietnam was finally under total communist control. The new Vietnamese government for all of Vietnam arrested more than 300,000 South Vietnamese who had cooperated with the Americans and the capitalists in South Vietnam, often tortured and killed.

The debacle of American involvement in Vietnam changed the way that Americans thought about their own government. Americans lost trust. Increased levels of anger and divisiveness emerged between different political factions in the United States.

A brutal communist regime controlled the reunified Vietnam. American prisoners of war remained in captivity. After the Vietnam War ended, Congress limited the powers of the American Central Intelligence Agency, passing new laws defining what the CIA could and could not do.

Excessive spending on the Vietnam War, combined with other American expenditures around the world, caused severe inflation in the United States. The American government had printed money to pay for the war without having sound reason to do so, causing devaluation of the dollar, and runaway inflation of prices and wages, which hurt the lower and middle classes the most. The purchasing power of every American citizen fell, as food and supplies cost much more. The effects of the American government overspending began to appear towards the end of the Vietnam War, with greater inflation taking place years after American spending for the Vietnam War had ceased. The effects of inflation badly hurt America's economy for more than 10 years in the 1970s and early 1980s. Inflation returned to more manageable levels by 1984 after the American Federal Reserve bank raised interest rates extremely high until the financial markets stabilized as the American government stopped recklessly printing money.

When the war was over, the conflict claimed the lives of millions of Vietnamese, as well as the lives of 75,000 American soldiers. Many thousands of Americans had been wounded and disabled by fighting in the war.

The greatest damage did not arise from American involvement in Vietnam. The majority of harm came from America's leaders escalating the war from 1966 onwards, in the face of convincing evidence that American efforts to win the war could not succeed. If there had been an earlier open discussion of the true facts of the war on the ground in Vietnam, American voters would have forced their leaders to begin withdrawing in 1966. Short-sighted decision-making of American leaders, together with the failure to pay attention to reliable information from advisors, led to bad decisions, and prevented America from changing course. Despite substantial evidence that America's efforts were fruitless and futile, American leaders continued to send soldiers into combat who were wounded and died, their families shattered.

It is not the American people who are to blame. Rather, leaders in government, in private industry and in the military are responsible for the Vietnam disaster. America supported a corrupt government in South Vietnam, which disadvantaged its own people. When investigators and reporters revealed true information about Vietnam, unprincipled American leaders claimed this was communist propaganda. The American government claimed that only ignorant, misguided, and unpatriotic people supported the notions that the Vietnam War was unwinnable, that the American presence in Vietnam was harming American interests.

LESSON 31: *When representatives of one side act out of personal self-interest, and against the valid interests of their own side, bad decision-making is likely.*

When President Johnson fabricated an excuse to bomb North Vietnam by falsely accusing the North Vietnamese of attacking an American warship, the North Vietnamese knew that this was an act of deception, committed by leaders who would use any ends to justify the means to obtain a goal. Settlement of any dispute becomes more difficult when one side loses trust due to the unprincipled actions of the other side.

America involved itself in a lengthy Vietnamese civil war which, without American intervention, would have ended with the same consequences: a communist government coming to power in Vietnam. Without American involvement, the nations affected could have avoided 10 years of highly destructive war. In fairness however, we have the advantage of hindsight, which was not available to American leaders in power at the time. It is incontestable, however, that powerful American leaders intentionally deceived the American voters. These American leaders were willing to continue to spill the blood of Americans and Vietnamese, despite awareness that there was little chance for a positive outcome to the fighting.

Ironically, the failure to be honest about the war in Vietnam, and the failure to stop the fighting much sooner, tarnished the reputations of these American leaders, much more than did their honest mistakes. The consequences of American involvement were worse than the problems that American leaders were trying to solve.

LE DUAN
(Public Domain Image)

Unknown to most Americans, Le Duan was second in command to Ho Chi Minh, the leader of North Vietnam. In charge of the underground communist forces in South Vietnam, Le Duan was the primary commander of the communist forces after Ho Chi Minh became ill and died in 1969.

He had fought to establish communism in Vietnam for decades prior to the Vietnam War. Educated in French colonial schools, he co-founded the Indochina Communist Party, and worked to overthrow the French government in Vietnam. More militant than Ho Chi Minh, Le Duan was a fierce supporter of communism. He did not hesitate to sacrifice the lives of his own people to create a fully independent, unified Vietnam with a communist government.

Le Duan recognized that America's support of the corrupt puppet government of South Vietnam was America's "Achille's Heel." Masterminding the Tet Offensive, he shortened a war that had already gone on far too long by breaking the American will to win in South Vietnam.

After the departure of American forces from Vietnam, Le Duan hoped that the common people of Vietnam would take a greater role in helping the new government to succeed. He did not anticipate that the per capita income of the Vietnamese people would decrease after the war ended. A considerable number suffered from poor health and malnutrition. New wars erupted between Vietnam with Cambodia and with China, creating further stress on the new communist Vietnamese government and its people. By the end of 1980, the inflation of the Vietnamese currency was 100% per year.

Disappointed by the difficulties he had encountered attempting to rebuild the economic and agricultural infrastructure of post-war Vietnam, Le Duan's ideology had prevented him from negotiating with capitalist American leaders to obtain a better post-war outcome. Despite winning a victory over America, Vietnam's communist leaders had extreme difficulties governing their people, while transitioning Vietnam's capitalist system to a functioning communist system. As time passed, severe unemployment continued. There were insufficient funds to provide food and care for the millions of orphans left from the war. In the decade following America's departure, Vietnam fought in two expensive and deadly wars with its neighbors. Then as a last resort, Le Duan finally gave in and limited Vietnam's independence, making a deal with the Soviets to preserve his communist government. His critics accused Le Duan of having sacrificed Vietnam's sovereignty.

Vietnam's extreme needs following the war were typical: wars usually leave both sides worse off than if they avoided further conflict through negotiation. Over the years, Vietnam's communism became more capitalistic and created trade and tourism relationships with America. This practical result illustrates the transitory nature of war, and the need to anticipate what the landscape will look like long after the war is over.

PART 5: Conclusions

The future depends on so many distinct factors. If a particular battle were won or lost, would that have made a difference? Who knows what person or what event might have changed everything? Although there is no way to accurately predict the future, it is important to consider some "What ifs":

If Britain and its American colonies agreed to a pre-war settlement in 1775, would this have prevented the later conflicts over slavery and helped to avoid the carnage of the American Civil War? Britain outlawed slavery in the early 1800s. If the Americans and the British had remained allied, instead of splitting apart in the American Revolution, it is likely that America would have outlawed slavery at the same time that it ended in Britain. The British eliminated slavery through reimbursement of the slave owners for the economic value of the loss of their slaves. If America had remained part of the British Empire, it is probable that a similar solution could have worked in America. Fear of losing a fight with the combined forces from Britain and the Northern Colonies would have prevented the Southern States from disputing the end of slavery.

Today, we take for granted that America is a superpower, but if the Confederacy had survived and America had split into two or more separate nations, what would the world look like today? Would the Nazis have conquered Europe without a unified America to help fight against the Germans during World War II? Imagine the potential world-wide negative consequences, had the Confederacy been successful in splitting the United States into two separate countries.

It is possible to argue that the Civil War provided a good outcome, as fighting the war gave the leaders of the South opportunities to make mistakes, which led to the complete abolition of slavery only 5 years after the Civil War started. If a pre-war settlement agreement relating to slavery avoided fighting the Civil War, slavery might have remained legal many years longer than it did. The problem with this argument is that it is difficult to say that it is preferable for a million people to die or suffer grievous injuries in fighting a war and weigh those consequences against a possible outcome of a pre-war settlement agreement between North and South, which might have extended the misery and injustice of slavery upon millions of people for an unknown length of time.

As mediators, we ascribe to the notion that it is better to accept the known outcome of a settlement agreement rather than proceed to an unknown outcome by fighting. When we say that one side or the other made mistakes in their negotiation or in their failure to negotiate, we view that choice from the perspective of that side, not from the perspective of what is best for the world. Making judgments about what was or is the best outcome for the world is beyond the skill of mediators. We must leave that to the philosophers, religious leaders, scientists, psychiatrists, and others whose capabilities far exceed our own.

Successful leaders must be careful when making decisions, as earlier successes may breed false confidence. It is no coincidence that leaders in Britain, the most powerful country in the world during the second half of the Eighteenth Century, and the leaders in America, the most powerful country in the world during the second half of the Twentieth Century, all acted against their own nations' interests, when it was unnecessary to do so.

Once firmly established in power, leaders may risk failure due to closing their minds, often forgetting the ways of thinking that brought their nations to power in the first place. Closed mindsets prevent the consideration of key information. Unfounded assumptions are usually based upon the failure to obtain the best information, which leaders can weigh before acting. Often, when one side discloses its best arguments, this is useful to the other side. Regardless of the source, all sides should carefully consider available information before walking away from negotiations.

Britain's leaders envied the prosperity of the American colonies. Yet, no leaders of Parliament traveled to America as the conflict with Britain increased, to see what was happening in America first-hand. It was a mistake for the members of Parliament to make decisions about the American colonies from the safety of their home nation, without the perspective and understanding derived from first-hand observation.

The American Revolution proved that a democratic union of states could be successful. Less than a century after the American Revolution, the Civil War tested whether this democratic union could maintain itself and reunite after a number of States attempted to break away to form their own separate nation.

Southern leaders might have avoided war if they had carefully considered what might go wrong. They believed France would support the Confederacy based upon France's support of the American Revolution. They did not sufficiently weigh the risk France might not cooperate. They did not consider the possible outcomes of secession. They failed to anticipate that refusal to export cotton to Britain would have the opposite effect from their intention to force support of the Confederacy by Britain. Instead, misguided Southern demands alienated Britain, and at the same time, cut off the flow of money from the sale of cotton, which impaired the ability of the Confederacy to purchase weapons and supplies.

Similarly, if President Lyndon Johnson had traveled to Vietnam during the war, it is much more likely that he might have recognized the opportunity to change the American strategy before the war escalated. Johnson felt he had to continue what others had started before, without doing his own homework to adequately assess the situation. He was too focused on domestic politics within America to see that this international problem would be his undoing. President Johnson and other American leaders departed from American values. They showed little concern for the welfare of the Vietnamese people. American leaders misjudged how the North Vietnamese would respond to more American troops arriving in Vietnam and how the North Vietnamese would respond to continued heavy bombing. Concern with personal political ambitions drove policies which destroyed countless lives and wasted the money of American taxpayers, without producing any long-term benefit to America.

In contrast, President Lincoln frequently left Washington, D.C., during the Civil War, to meet with his generals near the battlefields. Lincoln was deeply involved and informed. His first-hand knowledge allowed him to promote effective Union generals when other generals were not winning battles. If Lincoln had made all his decisions from the safety of Washington, D.C., or if he had acted upon his own private interests, it is likely that the Civil War would not have ended well for the North. Moreover, Lincoln was consistent and kept his eye on what he wanted to accomplish, never wavering. He gathered the available information and was not afraid to make tough decisions, so long as the decisions were likely to maintain the Union and benefit the American people.

Once engaged in a fight, people tend to lose sight of what is important. They can act upon faulty assumptions and may not look for opportunities to stop the fighting gracefully. Even worse, when people are losing, they are likely to "double-down," committing much more of their resources to fighting, often creating disastrous consequences. During the Civil War, the leaders of the South caused their own problems by refusing to recognize steps needed to be taken to achieve their best outcome, such as raising taxes and initiating a draft earlier. As events went against the South, their leaders refused to change their thinking, and refused to accept that they were losing, eventually suffering consequences much worse, from their perspective, than they ever imagined to be possible before the first shots were fired upon Fort Sumter.

Even though the majority of people may want to negotiate an acceptable solution rather than fight a war, a small minority from one side can hijack their entire side, using propaganda or terroristic actions, dragging their side into a landscape that cautious people would just as soon avoid. This was true with the American Revolution, instigated by the merchant class in the Colonies. Poor decision-making by the British leaders played into the hands of the American merchants. British obstinacy allowed these merchants to paint the British as evil, eventually convincing the majority of Colonials that war was the only solution.

Even worse than when uninformed leaders blithely proceed to fight, disinformation from bad actors may fan the flames of war, for their personal motives, often contrary to the best interests of their own people.

Wars also ignite when leaders disadvantage one part of their nation's population, making them second-class citizens. Not surprisingly, the freedom of people to control their own lives is a major theme of these American wars. It is not unusual for groups of people to be so motivated to control their own circumstances, that they will engage in risky fighting, knowing that the odds of victory are not good, knowing that their death and destruction may result.

Success in stopping wars requires convincing leaders and the common people of nations that their ideas of justice, that their ideas of the way the world works, or most importantly, that their predictions about how the future may unfold, may be unreliable. When people advocating war are zealous, it may be impossible for them to listen to reason. War is unavoidable when one side is convinced that war is the best path. Although zeal is important for winning wars, all combatants are at risk for failure, due to the potential for chaos, uncertainty, and luck, good or bad.

After experiencing the horrors of war, even zealous advocates of fighting may open their minds to accepting a solution to stop the fighting. The best that we can hope for is that leaders will be more receptive to ideas and rational arguments to help them be more flexible, consider all information and weigh potential solutions to help reach settlement agreements.

Leaders who tell lies impair their credibility and weaken their power to influence outcomes. Great leaders surround themselves with people who are good advisors, not just acolytes who always say "yes" out of fear of contradiction. A great leader knows that he or she is only human, that it is easy to make mistakes. To be their best, leaders need to hear accurate assessments of the potential consequences of their actions, both good and bad. Paying attention to good advisors and carefully listening allows leaders to have a better chance to make the right choices for their nations.

Integrity is strength: Most historians regard Abraham Lincoln as the best of our Presidents, due to his integrity. He was not two-faced. He never lied to the American people. He pursued the interests of America and had little regard for his own comfort and well-being, more concerned with doing the right thing than anything else. The integrity of Southern leaders failed when they closed their minds to the obvious, that Black Americans were human beings, entitled to all

Constitutional rights of life, liberty, and to be able to pursue happiness. Southern Planters did not seek the common good. They fought to remain rich by maintaining the practice of slavery, in spite of its evils.

If after learning the details of his decision-making and the quality of Lincoln's leadership, people still want to make arguments about Lincoln lacking morality and character, let them state the actual facts and circumstances supporting such arguments, instead of making conclusory and unsubstantiated allegations, in order to sway public opinion against this key American leader who managed to reunify America and end slavery, in spite of incredibly high odds of failure. Let those commentators show their own resumes as to what they have accomplished in their own lives, before presuming to play critic of such a great and effective leader as Lincoln.

It is amazing how the integrity of people may be more flexible where their own pocketbooks are concerned. British leaders were thinking of their own pocketbooks when they tried to extract more money from the Colonials. Southern planters knew that the end of slavery would reduce their profits. In the 1960s, the leaders of America were concerned about the profitability of American corporations, campaign contributions and re-election when they continued their interference with the operations of the government of South Vietnam.

In all wars, some people act admirably, most people act in their self-interest, and a lesser number of bad actors behave despicably, just like human beings everywhere have acted and will act in the future. The Founders designed the American Constitution to limit the power of bad actors, through the use of checks and balances of power among the Executive, the Legislative and the Judicial branches of government. When the voters identify bad actors, the voters must elect new representatives, guided by American values, in order for the American system of representative democracy to work at its best.

Great leaders tend to position themselves to take advantage of unforeseen changes that luck brings. Through unshakable moral stance, good instincts, patience and common sense, great leaders can take twists of fate and use them to advantage. By anticipating the possibility of change, then quickly adapting when change allows, leaders are likely to obtain better outcomes.

Before wars start, people may not consider the effects that war will have on their everyday lives. Human nature tends to take present circumstances for granted. We may not consider the important resources we use in our daily lives when they are stable and do not require immediate attention. We tend to assume that there always will be plenty of food, hot water, heat, electricity, and telephones, but war threatens all of these. War can shut down the electricity, turn off the heat and water, and deprive us of food. It makes sense that people use their brain power to focus on where the trouble is at a given time. Why worry about something that is not broken? But war always threatens and wastes basic resources. People need to keep in mind the negative consequences of war as motivation to reach out for solutions to conflicts before the fighting starts, when opportunities to settle wars present themselves.

These American wars demonstrate the challenges of a continually changing world. Effective problem-solving, acting within the law, guided by the principles in the American Constitution and the Bill of Rights, is the best course. Leaders must avoid law-breaking, name-calling, lying, and personal attacks if we are going to limit the risk of war.

For practical reasons, throughout its history, America's desire for trade and political alliances has taken precedence over encouraging other countries to choose representative democracy. American tolerance of other forms of government is understandable because America needs to build alliances with other nations, regardless of their form of government. When Americans needed help, they were not choosy about what type of government offered help. America should not upset the world order with misguided and clumsy attempts to convert other nations to the American style of democracy. To the contrary, it is in America's best interest to set an example of how well the American form of representative democracy can work, so that other leaders and other peoples may eventually embrace American values, after seeing the consistent prosperity and security which the American system of government provides.

It is typical, once any war is over, that opposing sides develop better relations over time, so long as the settlement arrived at to end the particular war was fair to both sides. A little over 80 years ago, Germany and Japan became enemies of America in World War II. Now all three nations are engaged in alliances providing mutual protection. When most American wars ended, normal relations eventually returned; "Us and Them", "Good and Bad" no longer apply.

Despite remaining resentment in the South over the destruction caused by the Civil War, America remains unified in more ways than it is divided. The current divisions in American politics have little to do with the historical conflict between Northern and Southern states.

There will always be wars. The key to maintaining national integrity is to fight in wars only when absolutely necessary, without straying away from our principles, aggressively striving to end the fighting at the earliest possible time. Diplomacy and negotiation will be effective in resolving conflicts between nations because all sides benefit by avoiding war. When diplomacy and negotiation cannot work, then nations must fight wars fiercely and intelligently, with the end in mind, settling the situation as soon as practicable.

Individual initiative, risk-taking, invention and hard work are the foundation of the American way of life. These American attributes have provided the opportunity to obtain prosperity. America grew more powerful as wealth accumulated due to the individual efforts of its citizens to better their own circumstances. People throughout the world continue to emigrate to America to have the chance to enjoy its freedoms and potential for prosperity.

One of the reasons the American style of capitalism produces such strong financial results is that the American people are free to engage, to innovate and create, all of which are dependent on freedom of speech, freedom to associate and freedom from government oppression. In America, there is no king, nor any top-down totalitarian system that tells Americans what they will do for a living. No system tells them where to live or how to spend their time.

America's strength is its flexibility in taking innovative ideas from other cultures and making them a part of American culture. International trade is a two-way street: Aldi, Cappuccino, Lattes, Sushi, Kim Chee, and Pho have all become part of American culture. McDonald's and Kentucky Fried Chicken are ambassadors of America world-wide. At the same time, America should be quick to reject bad ideas from other cultures, such as religious intolerance and controlled speech, which America's founders wisely rejected long ago.

America's power is based upon the positive results it provides for its people. America's prosperity allows it to maintain the highest military strength on Earth, essential for the security of its people. Representative democracy will increase around the world as America keeps proving that its form of representative democracy builds superior economies which can fund military strength to guard freedom and protect the people.

Interference with the internal operations of foreign nations impairs America's interests and reputation. When America unfairly uses brute power to subjugate the people of other countries, for the benefit of

American economic interests, these actions threaten the spread of democracy.

Immigrants come to America because of the opportunities and success that the American system provides without regard to social standing, race, or religion. Abandoning American ideals when dealing with foreign countries is antithetical to America's twin promises of opportunity and freedom. The message of America to other nations needs to be that, if you choose to run your nation like we run our nation, you will be better off. The people of other nations need to make their own decisions. America needs to only show the world how well the American system can function. Seeing American economic strength, citizens of other countries should want to copy the American system of government, at least in part, because America has fewer limitations on personal and financial growth than most places on Earth.

America should encourage all people throughout the world to possess the individual freedoms that Americans enjoy, including the freedom to hold fair elections within their countries. But it is the task of those people to forge their own futures. Supporting the American way of life does not mean imposing the will of American leaders upon other peoples or upon the leaders of other countries. Nor does it mean that America should interfere with communist governments, fascist governments, or monarchical governments. To the contrary, America will remain more powerful if other governments of the world trust American integrity.

American leaders have succeeded by developing and maintaining consistent relationships with other countries for mutual security and economic growth. America's positive relationships with other nations have fostered political stability, regardless of the type of political systems under which those nations operate. Poor decision-making for short-term gain sets America back. Sustaining American integrity is essential. America's word must be its bond.

The preservation of long-term political stability in America highlights the value of American leaders taking the long view with regard to decision-making. What will work going forward in the foreseeable future is important. We live in a constantly changing world. The real questions are two-fold: how to preserve quality of life, considering the needs of people in a changing world. That does not mean embracing a nostalgic view of the past, only to be disappointed by the inevitable changes the future will bring.

Intelligent and experienced leaders made mistakes in not avoiding or limiting these American wars. Looking back at the mistakes and the opportunities demonstrated in these difficult conflicts will guide us in moving forward.

Hope for the Future

The March of Folly, a book written by historian Barbara Tuchman, explores how, throughout world history, political leaders have often acted against their own interests.

Barbara Tuchman writes that, in both the War of the American Revolution and the War in Vietnam, "preconceived fixed attitudes," contrary to "common sense, rational inference and cogent advice", were foolishly embraced. Leaders tended to rely on the ideas they started out with, and stagnated mentally, refusing to acknowledge that changes in circumstances required flexible thinking to be able to adapt to meet the challenges caused by change. Without the ability to listen and learn from new information, leaders tended to pursue a path to failure, rather than change course. Barbara Tuchman calls this type of thinking "protective stupidity." She details examples which caused the failure of governments throughout history. She notes that circumstances may overburden these leaders with "too many subjects and problems in too many areas of government to allow solid understanding of any of them" with too little time to consider each of them.

She concludes that the most important qualities for leaders are "character" and "moral courage." She writes, "The problem may not be so much a matter of educating officials for the government as educating the electorate to recognize and reward integrity of character and to reject ersatz ("inferior quality") leadership."

Too much discussion in America today has its foundation in partisan politics, with opposing sides decrying the stupidity, cupidity, and evil motives of each other, instead of seeking to clarify where we all agree and seeking to find common ground. We need clear thinking and discussion. We should discourage polarizing political partisanship, which is counterproductive to the interests of all people. Creating fear among one's own supporters by accusing the political opposition of bad motives is counterproductive. Voters should demand that leaders seek consensus with the opposition, wherever possible, limiting conflict and avoiding the "Us or Them" mentality.

If they lack knowledge of the facts, voters are at the mercy of the propagandists, who retain their power through simplification, falsification, and obfuscation. Familiarity with circumstances of past wars should help reveal when current political leaders today are not telling the truth, where a small number of powerful people assert false information, attempting to hijack the voters with emotional appeals and untruths.

Common people with little ability to choose their own fates have fought in wars throughout history. A better future for the common people depends on them being sufficiently informed so as to cast their votes in the manner most likely to provide them with a better future.

The political problems in America today are just as pressing as they were in 1776. In political disputes, often there is no obvious "right" answer. People tend to look for the solutions that they see are "right," making their choice about what they see as the best path for living going forward. The best solutions, however, depend upon reaching a consensus, if possible, about the "right choices" for America going forward, which means anticipating the future needs of all Americans, as well as working to fix current problems.

The lessons of history are important. Removing statues and monuments is silly, as it limits the information available to the people. We usually see this type of destruction in totalitarian regimes, when the new regimes erase the old as a tactic to maintain the power of the new regime. For example, in 2001, the Taliban blew up the enormous 150-foot-high ancient statues of Buddha carved into stone mountains in Afghanistan as being the work of infidels. Declared false idols by the

Islamic Mullahs, the leaders of the Taliban destroyed these important relics. Aren't we engaging in the same kind of close-minded destruction as the Taliban when we destroy historical statues in America because we do not like their history? Statues are reminders of the triumphs and the errors of the past. It is more difficult to avoid errors if we are unaware of our past. In his book, A Little History of the World, E.H. Gombrich wrote, "It is a bad idea to try to prevent people from knowing their own history. If you want to do anything new, you must first make sure you know what people have tried before."

Now, political censorship is on the rise in democracies, despite the protections for freedom of speech and freedom of expression. Political statements claiming that this leader or that leader is bad or was bad are not useful. Instead, let the next generation become aware of the facts of the past and then decide for themselves where criticism is due, if any is due, then move forward to solve the current problems. Blame is of little use. Finding solutions that can benefit all is particularly useful.

The voters need more clarity, not conclusory partisan attacks. Americans need more discussion on how to solve problems together as one people. We do not need composed situations, circulated in bad faith, to purposely manipulate public opinion. We need an accurate analysis of the pros and cons of potential solutions to current problems to help us decide how to cast our votes.

Notice how important the word "we" is. "We" is a word which will save the world. The definition of "We" is not just me and my family, my race, my people. "We" must include all races and all nations when we make our choices about the best path to solving problems.

Nations in conflict will reach solutions through respectful dialogue. Let us see if we can agree about what is important: making the right choices to guide the future of America and the rest of the world. Our soldiers will appreciate that future American leaders make careful assessments to avoid wars. American leaders must be sure that fighting is necessary to protect American interests before risking the health and lives of American troops. Capable leadership in America will provide stability and reduce conflict in the ever-changing world of the future.

THE END

NOTES

FORWARD: Russia and Ukraine

1.   This war, triggered by Russia in its attempt to impose a new government in Ukraine, is not unexpected as this sort of conflict has occurred frequently throughout history. Reading about the destruction caused by these American wars highlights the importance of resolving wars as soon as possible. America is throwing money into the Russia/Ukraine conflict without achieving progress toward a long-term goal, just as the American government did in Vietnam. Moreover, America cannot afford to borrow money to finance fighting across the globe. Recall that France borrowed to finance the American Revolution and was later forced to raise taxes on the common people of France, which led to the disaster of the French Revolution. What unforeseen disaster will profligate spending bring to America? Of course, Americans worry about stopping Russian aggression, but the best way to do that is to help negotiate a settlement. America must demand that Ukraine begin negotiating with Russia in good faith to resolve the dispute, or America will reduce the flow of money to the Ukrainian government. Russia will likely gain some of the disputed territory, which is the only way to stop the fighting and bring long-term peace to the region. The current stalemate risks unforeseen events that could go badly for all involved. Stephen Kotkin's videos about this war on YouTube should be persuasive, explaining the need to "win the peace" with a deal providing long-term stability to that region through negotiation toward resolution.

2.	It is extremely hard to learn anything without becoming immersed in the subject. In law school, we read legal court decisions to understand how the facts of disputes are prerequisites to understanding how the legal decisions were reasoned to resolve these disputes. To be able to learn the principles to help stop the fighting, you have to first understand the facts of past conflicts. People like to hear stories, so I attempted to arrange the stories of the key facts and circumstances of these disputes in chronological order.

3.	Human psychology plays a major role in disputes. I was lucky to have taken the time during my "gap year" after college before going to law school to read a large number of books relating to psychology. It is important to be inquisitive, to be a detective of sorts, to be able to understand human motivations, to figure out how to help people. I did not list any psychology books as resources, as I have little recollection of all the psychology books which assisted my understanding. B.F. Skinner's <u>Beyond Freedom and Dignity</u> opened my eyes in the beginning. Steven Pinker's <u>How the Mind Works</u> was influential more recently. Most of all, practical experience dealing with people caught up in conflicts was the most important foundation for my education in negotiation and settlement.

4.	I have only provided fundamentals to help the reader see the process, and to learn how to act at a mediation. There is no magic here. There are many books about negotiation, recommending many distinctive styles and objectives. It is good to read a number of different books to find out which styles of negotiation appeal to you.

5. Many people dislike the process of negotiation. It is a personality thing. Others, like me, really like it. I was always pleased and surprised how quickly problems faded away if people made sincere efforts to solve them. Clarity in communication cannot be overvalued in this process.

PART 1: Negotiation and Settlement Fundamentals

6. The major takeaway from history was that the 1600s were incredibly bloody throughout Europe and America, due to religious wars, trade wars and colonialism. The extent of violence and cruelty exhibited during the 17th Century is shocking. Russell Shorto's book Amsterdam and Alan Taylor's book American Colonies describe a level of inhumanity that is unimaginable, to me at least.

7. Psychologist Jordan Peterson has expressed an important observation that most people are capable of the worst sorts of behavior, if placed in certain circumstances, war being one of them. Controlling this dark shadow found in most human minds requires adhering to the boundaries of law and acceptable behavior to maintain peace and order within our societies.

PART 2: The American Revolution: Lost Opportunities

8. Natural curiosity is a great motivator. As a practicing litigator, learning about the claims made in a lawsuit made me want to find out what really happened, as far as anyone could say, based upon physical

evidence and the testimony of witnesses. But a practicing lawyer works on a limited number of cases at one time, and these cases can go on for several years, sometimes decades. One of the reasons I became a mediator was the opportunity to attempt to resolve a substantial number of disputes in a brief period of time. I relished the challenge of understanding, then quickly resolving disputes which might otherwise continue for years. More often than not, successful mediation ended the disputes, usually in a win-win result for both sides. It is rewarding to help people move forward with their lives, as their worries over these disputes end.

9.   The creation of the democratic republic of the United States was lucky. The energetic and highly educated Founding Fathers created a lasting form of government designed to balance the needs of all Americans. The design of the American Constitution has helped to resolve the types of problems which had previously toppled other governments. Not only did the Founding Fathers successfully create a stable government to provide for the welfare of all of the American people, but they added unequivocal protection of the rights of all individuals in the Bill of Rights. The Founding Fathers also anticipated that future events might require changing the design of the American government, so long as most of the American people agree to make these changes.

10.   Most standard high school courses teaching American history discuss what events happened and when they happened, but give oversimplified explanations regaining why events happened. My personal experience was that the history textbooks presented the reasons for war from a single "accepted" perspective. We were told that America was always right, and that everybody agreed about what had started a war and why it ended. Nobody ever taught us the true

circumstances or admitted that America had made serious mistakes. Nobody ever presented America in an unfavorable light. Did the federal, state, and local governments of America control the content of American history courses to minimize scrutiny of their governments, or was the oversimplification designed to promote unquestioning compliance with government messages? Is there a better explanation? I am curious to know the answer to that question.

11.   In response to a question he was asked at a lecture, the highly-educated writer and political commentator Christopher Hitchens' named Theodore Draper's Revolutionary war book, A Struggle for Power, as the one book he would recommend, if he had to pick one book for people to read about history of any type. I was impressed with Theodore Draper's clarity and insights in that book. After reading it, I felt much more comfortable knowing what the conflict with Britain was about and why the war was fought.

PART 3: The American Civil War: Refusal to Change

12.   There was tremendous change in America in the early 1800s, with the rate of change increasing with the technological explosion of the Industrial Revolution. When we consider the rapid pace of change in the centuries since then, we realize the need for our governments to accommodate change to ensure the continued economic success which funds American prosperity and security. If I could bring back one person from the past to show him or her how different America is today compared with America in 1776, I would pick Benjamin Franklin. He would be amazed at everything: Paved roads with cars moving at unimaginable speeds, electric lights, music and videos on

demand, instant communication around the world, supermarkets, air and space travel, government safety nets, amazing medicines, and the great increase in life expectancy. I am sure he would not be surprised that we take all of these benefits for granted and that we are no happier than people in 1776. Benjamin Franklin would appreciate how practical America has been in making the lives of the average American more secure. At the same time, if Benjamin Franklin learned about the destructive potential of nuclear weapons, he would surely insist that Americans must do everything possible to coordinate with other governments to accommodate the needs of other peoples' governments and help to solve their problems in a practical way, rather than risk the destruction of civilization.

13.　　I wanted to tell the truth about how many white people were prejudiced against black people when the Civil War began, because it shows how Lincoln, who hated slavery, had been placed in an impossible predicament as President but somehow charted a course that led to freedom for all slaves less than 5 years after the war started. I also wanted Americans to be able to acknowledge how wrong many of us were at the time of the Civil War, and how good it is now that we are much closer to having a color-blind society, which will make America more powerful and will help individual American citizens of all ethnicities and from different cultures to find success, working together.

14.　　The financial success of Southern Leaders generated their arrogance. Happy to be wealthy, they believed in their inherent superiority. Their pride led to their downfall. Along with many others who are proud to be American, we must always remember that superior outcomes are based upon effort, practical problem solving and good luck. People all over the world are the same, and all deserve our respect and assistance when in need, just as we deserve their respect and assistance when we are in need, so that we may all have good outcomes.

15.   The stories of these key people highlight the unpredictability of events that nobody anticipated. Looking at the current war in Ukraine, the success of Ukrainian leader Volodymyr Zelenskyy was unexpected and added to the strong Ukrainian resistance. What other unexpected events will shift the course of this war? Wait and see.

PART 4: The Vietnam War: A Study in Hubris

16.   Max Hastings book Vietnam: An Epic Tragedy is a wonderful read, despite its great length, which was required simply because there was so much material to work with. There are so many people, so many perspectives, so much detail available from the contemporaneous documentation of what happened. I looked at other sources, but Max Hastings deserves great kudos for his efforts. It reveals the complexity of American governmental power, at the same time detailing how a few American leaders were able to take control of the Vietnam situation and sell the American people on a false narrative, until it all unraveled when the impossibility of an American victory was finally revealed. Today, more than 50 years later, we see that America is just as vulnerable, if not more vulnerable, to manipulation via disinformation, deep-fake videos, simplification, and emotional appeals, which keeps people from embracing practical solutions to the real problems which need solutions.

PART 5: Conclusions

17.   An excellent short book regarding conclusions which can be drawn from history is Will and Ariel Durant's <u>The Lessons of History</u>. These highly regarded historians became famous for writing an immense masterpiece of world history called <u>The Story of Civilization.</u> Edward R. Dougherty wrote an excellent review of <u>The Lessons of History</u>, which is currently posted on the website of the National Association of Scholars. The Durants authored this book to share the conclusions they had come to, after studying world history since the beginning of the written word. Their most important conclusion was that, when a civilization declines, it is because of the failure of its political or intellectual leaders to meet the challenges of change. The American people fight today against the challenges of communism, against intolerance and against attacks upon the freedom of its citizens. As the Durants advised, we need to select people as our leaders who will successfully meet "the challenges of change" going forward.

INDEX

RESOURCES

Beschloss, Michael, PRESIDENTS OF WAR THE EPIC STORY, FROM1807 TO MODERN TIMES © 2018 Broadway Books, New York.

Boorstin, Daniel J., THE AMERICANS THE COLONIAL EXPERIENCE, 1958, Random House, Inc.

Cartledge, Paul, DEMOCRACY: A LIFE, Audible Audiobooks, © 2016

Catton, Bruce, E.B. Long, Contributor, THE COMING FURY (THE CENTENNIAL HISTORY OF THE CIVIL WAR, VOLUME 1, Doubleday and Company, © 1961

Catton, Bruce, The Great Courses- THE CIVIL WAR, available on Audible.com

Catton, Bruce, GRANT MOVES SOUTH, © 1960, Little Brown and Company, Inc.

Chambers, Whitaker: WITNESS © 2014, Rengery History.

Desan, Suzanne S. LIVING THE FRENCH REVOLUTION AND AGE OF NAPOLEON, © 2013, The Teaching Company

Draper, Theodore, A STRUGGLE FOR POWER/ THE AMERICAN REVOLUTION, © 1996, Random House.

Durant, Will and Durant, Ariel, THE LESSONS OF HISTORY, Simon & Schuster, © 1968

Foote, Shelby; THE CIVIL WAR, VOLUMES 1-3, © 1991 Easton Press.

Gallagher, Gary W., The Great Courses-THE AMERICAN CIVIL WAR, available on Audible.com.

Gombrich, E.H., A LITTLE HISTORY OF THE WORLD, Yale University Press, © 2005

Goscha, Christopher, VIETNAM- A NEW HISTORY © 2017, Tantor Audio.

Guelzo, Alan C., The Great Courses-AMERICAN REVOLUTION, available on Audible.com.

Hastings, Max; VIETNAM AN EPIC TRAGEDY, 1945-1975, © 2018, Harper Collins.

Hedrick, Joan D., HARRIET BEECHER STOWE - A LIFE, © 1994 Oxford University Press.

Hitchens, Christopher, THOMAS PAINES' RIGHTS OF MAN, A BIOGRAPHY, © 2006, Atlantic Monthly Press.

Isaacson, Walter, BENJAMIN FRANKLIN: AN AMERICAN LIFE © 2004, Simon & Shuster.

Johnson, Dominic D.P, OVERCONFIDENCE AND WAR -THE HAVOC AND GLORY OF POSITIVE ILLUSIONS © 2004, Harvard University Press.

Kinser, Stephen, THE BROTHERS: JOHN FOSTER DULLES, ALLEN DULLES AND THEIR SECRET WORLD WAR, © 2013, Time Books, Henry Holt and Company, LLC.

Klooster, Wim, THE DUTCH MOMENT: WAR, TRADE AND SETTLEMENT IN THE SEVENTEENTH-CENTURY ATLANTIC WORLD, Cornell University Press, ©2016.

Kotkin, Stephen, ARMAGEDDON AVERTED: THE SOVIET COLLAPSE, 1970-2000, Audible Audiobook, Tantor Audio © 2001.

McPherson, James M.; BATTLE CRY FOR FREEDOM - THE CIVIL WAR ERA, © 1988, Oxford University Press, Inc.

Roberts, Andrew, et. al.; THE LAST KING OF AMERICA: THE MISUNDERSTOOD REIGN OF GEORGE III, © 2021 Penguin Audio

Short, Russell, Amsterdam: A HISTORY OF THE WORLD' S MOST LIBERAL CITY, Vintage Reprint Edition, © 2014

Talib, Nassim Nicholas, FOOLED BY RANDOMNESS: THE HIDDEN ROLE OF LUCK IN LIFE AND IN THE MARKETS, © 2005 Random House Trade Paperback

Taylor, Alan, AMERICAN COLONIES: THE SETTLING OF NORTH AMERICA (VOUME 1, PENGUIN HISTORY OF THE UNITED STATES   Penguin Books © 2001)

Taylor, Alan, AMERICAN REVOLUTIONS, A CONTINENTAL HISTORY, 1750-1804, © 2016, W.W. Norton & Company, New York and London.

Tuchman, Barbara W., THE MARCH OF FOLLY FROM TROY TO VIETNAM, © 1984, Alfred A. Knopf, New York.

Willink, Jocko, Podcast 31, with Echo Charles, reviewing book "FOUR HOURS IN MY LAI" © 1993 by Michael Bilton and Kevin Sim, published by Penguin Books.

ABOUT THE AUTHOR

Bob Worden, Esq. is an award-winning Arbitrator and Mediator with extensive expertise in understanding, explaining and resolving complex conflicts. His intensive studies regarding the facts and circumstances which led to American wars have allowed Bob to create How to Stop Wars and Save the World, which teaches everyday people about what really happened which led to these American wars, and why all wars should be settled as soon as possible. Everyone involved or affected by wars needs to learn these lessons, to help avoid, or at least limit, the terrible consequences of war.